JUST BECAUSE I'M
AUTISTIC
DOESN'T MEAN I'M STUPID

A MOTHER/
DAUGHTER STORY
*of defying the odds and being
successful in their lives*

SHARI L. COLE &
BRITTANY J. COLE

*Real-life information, experiences and survival tips
we wish we had back when we really needed it*

Printed in the United States of America
Cole, Shari
Cole, Brittany
    Just Because I'm Autistic Doesn't Mean I'm Stupid
    Library of Congress Cataloging-in-Publication Data
    ISBN: 978-1-943784-42-4

Disclaimer
This book is designed to share insights into the life of a mother, her daughter who was diagnosed with autism as a toddler and everything that came after. It is sold with the understanding that the publisher and author are not engaged in rendering medical, legal or other professional services. If medical, legal or other expert assistance is required, please seek the services of a specialist.

The purpose of this book is to educate, motivate, inspire, entertain and support. The author and Vervante shall have neither liability nor responsibility to any person or entity with respect to any loss or damage caused, or alleged to have been caused, directly or indirectly, by the information contained in this book.

DEDICATION

To Matthew, Brittany's champion... the brother she played with, the brother who shared his friends with her, the brother who watched over her since the day she was born, the brother she went to for advice, the brother who was always there for her and never treated her differently.

And to my son, an old soul who has always been good to me and good for me – and instrumental to our success.

*"What is normal? Normal is boring.
Special is colorful and interesting!"*

"There is no such thing as perfection, as perfection is not normal. To have imperfections is what makes a person interesting."

Shari Cole

TABLE OF CONTENTS

ACKNOWLEDGEMENTS

Julie, you are a true friend and a sister of my heart. We've been through it all together, and I don't know if I'd have made it without you.

Dad, my Music Man, thank you for helping me see that the glass is never empty, it's overflowing.

Mom, you gave me hope when I felt hopeless. You hold no judgments and told me to make good choices in my life – as if you don't, they will follow you until the day you die. You are my best friend, my mom, and I adore you.

Lori, you're my strength, my confidant and my rock. I couldn't get through this life without you.

Stacy, you inspire me and give me that boost when I need it, both spiritually and emotionally.

INTRODUCTION

BRITTANY:

When I heard that mom was writing a book about me, I figured I should have my say, too.

Hi, I'm Brittany! When I meet people, I don't say, "Hi, I'm Brittany Cole, and I'm autistic!" That's just stupid. I want people to get to know me and like me for who I am, not what I am.

Once, when I was in Israel touring with a group of other kids my age, our guard heard me share that I was autistic. He approached me later and said that I didn't seem autistic. Then he asked what it meant to be autistic. Now there's a question I've heard so much in my life. So I told him how I'm considered to be on the mild end of the spectrum. And how people still struggle with how I seem on the surface and that they can't see my autism. Sometimes I wonder what they want me to do... wear a T-shirt that says it?

Instead, I explained all of my personal quirks, the endless therapies and the work I've done throughout my life to get where I am. I told him about how I have trouble making eye contact in a conversation. How I tend to interrupt often and have trouble carrying on a polite conversation. He laughed and said, "Oh, well, all Israelis are that way. You'll fit in well here."

While he was funny, it got me thinking. When people ask me what makes me unique, I don't immediately think of the autism. I'm unique because I'm an artist, a woman, an American, Jewish and autistic. These things play equal parts in making me who I am. Autism is not ALL of me but, yes, it's a definite part of what makes me unique and special. I'm really proud of being autistic and, while I'm not on the severe end of the spectrum, I feel like my accomplishments are painting a good image for other autistic kids – painting a hopeful picture for what's possible. Maybe not everyone who reads this book can do what I've done, but they can aspire to get there. They need to hear from me. And that's why I'm here!

SHARI:

On December 15, 1995, my best friend Julie broke the news to me that her husband had been diagnosed with advanced lung cancer. He passed away a few weeks later. A little bit after that, on January 18, 1996, I learned that my 2-year-old daughter Brittany had autism. My life instantly changed forever.

Some people call the death of a loved one an ending. Others say it's a transition to the next life. Looking back, I can see now that Brittany's diagnosis was a bit of both for me. I was overwhelmed with grief. The child we thought we had was gone forever, replaced with a "new" child that January day. Maybe it was the shock of all this happening at the same time, but for a while after that I felt like a ghost. I drifted through day-to-day life, existing in a continual state of shock, never really making any decisions, any choices for moving forward in our lives and dealing with what was going on. I really believe that there are few things in this world as earth-shattering as that moment when you receive a diagnosis like this. The scope of emotions is indescribable. The comfort I'm here to share with anyone in a similar situation is that everything else that happens after the diagnosis you know you can deal with, because you survived this moment.

Looking back, I really shouldn't have been that surprised. From the start, I knew there was something going on with Brittany that I couldn't explain. It was that gut feeling mothers have, I guess, but no one else seemed to notice. The more I tried to talk about it, the more people made me feel like I was losing it.

I couldn't stop calling my pediatrician to tell him, "I know something is wrong with my baby girl!" I just was never able to put my finger on it. After a year of persistent calls, he finally asked me to videotape the behaviors that were causing me concern so that he could see what I was talking about. He was probably hoping that I would finally see that there was nothing to worry about. Or that I would be unable to capture anything, and he could say, "I told you so."

That video changed our lives forever. It led us to the discovery of Brittany's autism. And to a whole new life as a mother like nothing I'd ever imagined. Back then, more than 20 years ago, the statistics were a lot different than they are today. Approximately 1 in 150 children was diagnosed on the autism spectrum. Now, according to 2014 CDC reports, the numbers are closer to 1 in 50 and rising. Back then, the amount of information and resources available for parents of autistic children was little to none. Now, you can't turn around without seeing a new support group, a new study, a new school or any number of resources for parents.

One thing that hasn't changed, though, are the emotions that every parent goes through. And the inevitable loneliness. For a parent, no matter how little or how much you know, it can be easy to find yourself emotionally walled in as you struggle to deal with your child's autism. I used to say that I wished there was another me around who could have told me what to do when I was going through this.

And that's why I wrote this book – to provide a sort of best friend's guide to life with an autistic child. An inside peek into my life... all the things I did wrong, all the things I did right, the struggles and the rewards, the unbearable loneliness and the lifelines I found that pulled me out of my emotional funks. And to know that no matter what, you can find a way, you will survive, and you are not alone! Because when it comes down to it, we all go through that feeling of being so utterly alone that no one else can possibly know what we feel... that no one else can understand or help us.

But that's just not true. We're in this together.

YOU'RE NOT ALONE.

This is for you.

Chapter
1.

Hi, I'm Autistic!

BRITTANY:

I didn't even know I was autistic until around 4th grade – I guess around 8 or 9 years old. We were reading an article in the newspaper about a brother helping a sister with autism. Mom said that we were like those kids, and I asked how. She said, "Because you are!" I am? I am what?

I was really confused and had no idea what she was talking about. The word "autism" didn't really mean much at the time; I'd never noticed anything different about us. But as I got older, I looked back and thought, "Oh, that's why" and understood what was going on.

The first time I was around a bunch of other autistic kids was a "WALK FOR AUTISM" sponsored by Autism Speaks at the Rose Bowl in Pasadena. We walked around a stadium. I saw some kids in wheelchairs, some supported by braces because they didn't have muscle tone to support themselves. Kids from all walks of life, all different neighborhoods and lots of different types of families. They all acted differently, looked differently... coming from so many places and showing such a big variety from all over the spectrum in one place. It was amazing to see.

For me, personally, I often feel like there are certain things happening around me that I can't master. And I know somewhere inside that I can't do certain things because of the autism. It's like hitting a wall. I can't explain it, but it's a feeling inside that I get.

When I meet people, I don't say, "Hi, I'm Brittany Cole. I'm autistic." I want them to know me and like me for who I am, not what I am. There's never been an occasion when it should matter that much.

SHARI:
I didn't know that Brittany was autistic right from birth, but there were a lot of little things during her first year that were warning signs for me. I had a lot of trouble breastfeeding because she was always flapping her hands, rocking and making repetitive movements of some kind or another. (I would later find out this is called stimming.) She wasn't vocal and didn't use any of the baby talk that her brother Matthew did, and

he was only a year older. It was nearly impossible to take her out of the house – she would scream, cry, throw massive tantrums and drive everyone crazy. We couldn't figure out what was wrong.

After a year of my pediatrician telling me that everything would eventually work out, I demanded that we test for something, anything. A mother always knows, and I knew that something was up with Brittany. The doctor gave in and asked me to make a video so that he could see what I was talking about. I recorded her movements, her moods and her surroundings, and I sent it in.

The very next day at our appointment, we were told.

"Brittany has autism."

We made an appointment to see a visiting neurologist who saw patients in our area once a month. He watched the video and examined Brittany. And on January 18, 1996, he told us that Brittany had all the characteristics of autism. To be exact, he said she was mildly autistic with medium-level obsessive-compulsive disorder (OCD).

Now I panic.

"What?! No, this can't be happening. What does this mean for her? For us? Why her? Why us? How could God let this happen to my innocent baby?"

Thoughts like this – and a million more – rolled through

my head. I hit the panic button hard. I couldn't breathe, I couldn't think, I couldn't form a coherent sentence. When I finally kicked my brain back into gear and voiced my questions and concerns to the neurologist, I found myself forced right back into the same position of being told I was overreacting.

This doctor who didn't know us, who didn't know my daughter, who only came into our area once a month, told me that I should do... nothing. He told me to wait six months to a year to "see if things change." I was mortified by his coldness, his lack of knowledge when I asked for more specific information about autism, the diagnosis and how to help Brittany.

I knew this wasn't right. I knew we needed to do something. When I dared to mention this, he said, "Excuse me, Shari, but I'm the doctor. She's my patient. And I know best."

When I heard that, the spinning stopped. I didn't know what I was going to do, but I did know that waiting and doing nothing was not an option. I became a warrior for my child. And I said to him, "Screw that! I'm the mom, and this is MY CHILD. I know what's best for her. And by the way, you're fired."

I took my daughter home and refused to wait for him or anyone else. I needed to be a warrior for my daughter. I needed to fight for her, not just wait to see what happened. A mother knows, right?

Once home, I got my address book out and started

calling people close to me. I reached out to family, friends and anyone I knew who might know something or someone in the autism world who could help us. I reached out to the connections I'd made during my career in the Hollywood entertainment industry. I reached out to everyone. I read every autism book I could get my hands on (big mistake; more on that in a minute). I started out really strong.

I was a warrior, and I was kicking ass and taking names – all on my own.

Honestly, reading every book about autism was probably one of the worst things I could have done, and I'm sharing this so that other parents don't make the same mistake I did. Not every book about autism is a good book. In fact, most of the books I was reading were either extremely clinical and difficult to understand or depressing. Or both.

These books were not about hope, happiness or success. They didn't tell me that I wasn't alone. They didn't break things down into steps that I understood. Instead, I was reading books filled with doom and gloom and all of the horrible things that my daughter may have to go through, sharing them in such exquisite detail that I found all hope being sucked out of me. They instilled fear and informed me that my child had no hope for happiness in her future. So I cried. And I cried some more.

I moved from autopilot mode into "cry-all-the-time" mode. The books made me cry. Talking to people about Brittany made me cry. Watching TV made me cry. I couldn't stop crying. So I started drifting. I would pull myself together enough to get my kids to preschool. I can't tell you what I did with my time in between, because I can't remember. I just felt blank. The books were feeding my fears: What if all of the dreadful things I'm imagining happen to Brittany? Will she ever be able to live alone, support herself, find love, have a family?

My sister Lori, who I leaned on and talked to almost every day, finally told me, "Enough! Stop reading those damn books! They're depressing you to the point where you can't function or think straight."

She was so right. I threw all of those sad, depressing, scary books away. I realized that I was no good to my family if I was in a constant state of tearful depression, so I decided to pull it together and fight the good fight as my daughter's advocate. My husband at the time agreed, and together we decided that my new job was to work with Brittany full time.

Until that time, I had a career as a producer in the movie industry. I put in the time, paid my dues and loved what I did. But I loved my kids more. And I knew I needed to be there for Brittany. I mean *really* be there, because I was quickly learning that no one else would be.

I soon found Lynn Koegel, an eminent psychologist who specializes in autism. She is well-known in the autism community and the author of several books about autism. Her caring, naturalistic approach to working with children on the autism spectrum appealed to me.

Dr. Koegel started out by videotaping Brittany to observe her behaviors and advise us on what the next steps were and what we needed to work on. Brittany was about 2 1/2 years old at this point. Dr. Koegel, who already had a very full practice, told me that she took Brittany on because she saw hope and knew that Brittany could be successful with some work. This was music to my ears, so we got to work – once we figured out which areas we needed to work on.

It was exhausting. Occupational therapy three days a week. Behavior modification three days a week. We worked on cognitive therapy. Brittany had therapists shadow and observe her in preschool and at home. Dr. Koegel, who was affiliated with UCSB at that point, sent her grad students to work with Brittany at our home north of Los Angeles, as well.

Even with all of this, I didn't see any progress over the year. I remember one exercise Dr. Koegel did with Brittany was to take a handful of M&Ms and ask Brittany to identify the colors by touching each one and saying what the color was. We worked and worked on it, but she never spoke. They also started using small animal figurines from the Littlest Pet Shop toys for repetitive motions (put them down, remove, replace, etc.). I didn't see any progress. I really started to worry. Brittany was almost 4.

I decided something dramatic was needed. We looked into a hard-core autism treatment program at UCLA.

The program was very intense, requiring Brittany and me to live near UCLA so that we could attend eight hours a day, seven days a week for 30 full days. I wasn't sure about it but felt like I had to do something to move forward.

Back then, insurance didn't help out with any of these programs. We were on our own to cover the fees associated with any programs for autism treatment. The program I was looking into at UCLA was expensive. In a move to find a way to afford it, Terry (my now ex-husband) and I met with his former wife to see if she would be flexible with alimony payments just for a little while so that we could afford this very expensive program. I can't begin to tell you how painful that was for both of us. She said no.

Then a miracle happened: Brittany passed the M&M test! She said blue for the blue one! And yellow for yellow! And green for green! Hallelujah!

Like Sleeping Beauty, Brittany finally woke up. It was as if the heavens opened, and angels started singing. My child spoke. She knows her colors! She knows M&Ms! I was overwhelmed, hysterically laughing and crying all at once. I called Terry, jubilant that we didn't have to borrow, beg and steal for that new program. I didn't have to move to UCLA for a full month.

Seventeen years later, and I can still remember clearly how great that day felt. It was like a dam broke loose. Once she found her voice, progress started, and we could all move forward.

Don't think I'm getting all woo-woo on you here but, looking back, I know that I was in the place I needed to be at the time I needed to be there to deal with what I had to face regarding Brittany's future. My career had given me the connections, friends, experience and resilience to deal with this – even though I didn't feel that way at the time. Looking back, I know that it was meant to be.

I also had to work through the guilt factor. Believe me, it doesn't take long to start down that path. I felt guilty about everything I did before, during and after my pregnancy. I drove myself nuts wondering if I had done something wrong. If things would have been different if I had made other choices. If I could blame Brittany's father's DNA for this... or that her father was over 45 when she was conceived. I'd read that this could be a contributing factor. Was it?

I drank some champagne very early in my pregnancy, before I even knew I was pregnant. Could that be the cause? Was there something in my family's genetic history that caused it? What about that water ski trip early in my pregnancy; maybe I did something then that caused it. How about those vaccines? Over-the-counter drugs? Too many cough drops when I was sick? The list went on and on.

This is natural. After all, we just want answers. But it's not a productive path, as there really are no answers. Sure, you're going to be emotional. A lot. And you're going to be angry. A whole lot more. But instead of wallowing and questioning and wondering, the most productive thing you can do is use that anger to put your warrior clothes on and go to battle for your child.

The day my sister told me to throw the books away was the day she helped me learn to focus on what needed to be done, day by day, and start moving forward for everyone. You don't know what the future will bring. Neither do your doctors, your therapists, your nosy neighbors or your catty frenemies. You can't predict the advances and breakthroughs and small miracles that can and will happen in the coming years, so get your warrior gear on, and keep at it.

I jumped into research mode to arm myself. I researched the crap out of the Americans with Disabilities Act (www.ada.gov) and the The Individuals with Disabilities Education Act (IDEA) (http://idea.ed.gov/) to learn what my rights and the rights of my child are. This is probably one of the strongest things I did that continues to help Brittany to this day. Don't assume that the doctors, therapists, teachers, school administrators and others who are in a position to help you will know what you are legally entitled to or will volunteer that information on their own.

For instance, under the Americans with Disabilities Act, your child has the right to attend the school of your choice, and you can even select her teachers. You can interview those teachers to decide. Each school year, I sat down with the special education teacher or counselors, and we worked out plans for who we thought the best teachers for Brittany were.

Make sure that your child has an Individualized Education Program, or IEP. In the United States, an IEP is mandated by the Individuals with Disabilities Education Act. The IEP is intended to help children reach educational goals more easily than they otherwise would. In all cases, the IEP must be tailored to the individual student's needs and must especially help teachers and related service providers understand the student's disability and how the disability affects the learning process. (I'll share more details on IEPs in Chapter 4.)

Every special education child is different and has different needs. Personally, I think it's important to keep kids on the autism spectrum mainstreamed so that they can rise to the occasion. If you hold them back or keep them segregated from the rest of the school, they will never progress. I regret to this day putting Brittany in a special ed math class. Now, as she nears her university graduation, she tells me the same thing.

She has never done well in math and blames it on the special education math classes we put her in. They progressed so slowly that she could never catch up with her peers, and she struggles to this day. On the other hand, we decided she should take every other class with the general population in high school. In each of those classes, she rose to the occasion – learned, progressed and grew – but not in math.

Looking back, I realize I was a bit of a tyrant walking into those meetings. I may have even been seen as a bitch at times, but at least I tried to do it in a graceful way. It all circles back to being that warrior for your child. What really matters is the end result – making sure your child is with the right people and given support that meets her needs and helps her succeed.

Hindsight is 20/20, right? I didn't just naturally figure all of this out by myself. Back then, no one really knew too much about autism, especially about the rights of children on the autism spectrum who attend public school. I was so lost that I had to hire an advocate to help me.

Andrea Lorant, an advocate and education consultant who practices in the Los Angeles and Ventura County areas, was a lifesaver. She helped me understand the rights that Brittany and I were due. And the best part? When she walked into an IEP meeting or any other meeting to address Brittany's needs, people would immediately start giving us what we wanted – not because they were afraid of her (well, maybe a little), but because they knew we were well-informed of our legal rights and that they were obligated to provide Brittany and me with the support and resources we sought.

Above all, I realized that every time I walked into a meeting, I needed to leave my emotions at the door and think of myself as the CEO of a business – the business of Brittany. I didn't always have an advocate to help me. And I quickly learned that I couldn't afford to be emotional during those meetings because people wouldn't hear me.

I realize not everyone has the ability to hire an advocate, but there are a lot of nonprofit community, government and online support groups that can help – or refer you to the person with the expertise you need. Look for organizations, support groups and educational resources in your area and online that fit your child's specific needs. I really love the organizations Autism Speaks (www.autismspeaks.org) and Talk About Curing Autism (TACA) (www.tacanow.org).

Whatever you do, don't withdraw – reach out!

And finally... I can't stress this enough: Stay focused on learning, growing and moving forward. Stop playing the coulda-woulda-shoulda game. Regrets will not help you, and they certainly won't help your child. Sure, it's normal to have regrets, but it's not productive to hold onto them. I'm not perfect, I still work on this too, but I know that we have to let regrets go and stop beating ourselves up over what could have been, would have been or should have been. My mom always said the past is the past; you can't go back, so stop trying.

Do the best you can, realize you're doing the best you can with what you have, and keep moving forward... warrior style!

Chapter
2.

Life with Autism

BRITTANY:

> Along with my blog, I also have a Twitter account that
> I'm pretty active on. I'm open about my experiences
> with autism, and I've had other kids reach out to me.

> For instance, one girl told me she loves to doodle and
> draw and really connected with me. It was sad because
> she told me she felt like her parents didn't like her...
> that she felt alone, as if she was on an island with no
> one who understood her, and everyone thought she
> was stupid because she was autistic. I realized as I
> talked to this girl how lucky I am. My mother never
> treated me any differently because I was autistic. She
> always expected the best from me and never let me
> slack. And I always knew I was loved.

I wanted to help this girl. I shared with her how I view having autism as good, kind of like X-Men super powers. Autistic kids are born with these powers, genetically different and often misunderstood, like the X-Men. But our differences can become an advantage once we learn how to use them.

I may not be as good at some things, but I'm really good at others, and I definitely have my strengths. Once I learned to focus on things in that light, autism seemed pretty cool.

I told her, "You'll always have people looking down on you, who think you can't understand certain things because you're autistic, but you have super powers as an autistic person. You're different, and that's OK. You don't think the same, and that's OK. Different is not bad, it's good!"

SHARI:
Brittany started a blog when she was in high school to give people an insider's look at the life of an autistic teen as well as a peek inside how she sees, addresses and reacts to situations in life – situations others rarely give a passing thought.

It's funny... as her mom, you would think I know it all, but as I read her blog, I've learned a lot about what she was seeing and feeling that I don't think I truly understood before. If you have an autistic child, I highly recommend reading through similar blogs written by other autistic children (check the resources section at the end of this book).

If your child is open to the experience, see if she is interested in keeping a journal or starting a blog. It's a great way to share her unique perspective while giving those of us around her a peek inside and some enlightenment on how we can better understand and support children with special needs like hers.

There's a saying about autistic kids: "If you've met one person with autism, you've met one person with autism." No two people with autism are alike. Although they share many similarities, each child is unique in the signs, behaviors and abilities he or she possesses.

There are so many little things no one warns you about when your child is diagnosed with autism. They focus on the big stuff but forget to tell you about how your child probably will have some OCD characteristics... that they might struggle their whole lives with keeping track of time... that they will have weird fixations and fetishes you'll have to learn to deal with.

For instance, no one told me that her shoes needed to be really snug – that it felt good to her to have her shoes tied really tight. Or that she wouldn't be able to sleep at night unless I tucked her sheets around her really, really tight, like a little cocoon. These were little things that made her feel safe and comfortable with the world. Heaven help me if I forgot them.

As Brittany was growing up, people often asked if she had "outgrown" her autism yet, like it was bed wetting or something that would eventually go away. You never outgrow autism. It's more that you trade one set of problems for another through each stage of life.

At first, you are the be-all, end-all, do-it-all-for-them person who is critical in helping them navigate through life. Then, as they mature, they become more self-aware. They develop an understanding of what and where their feelings come from as well as the ability to deal with those feelings on their own.

We're sharing Brittany's experiences here to give you a peek at what we saw and dealt with. Our hope is that some of what is shared will ring a bell, help you see that you're not alone and give you hope knowing that someone else went through the same things you're going through.

STIMMING

BRITTANY:

I had a bad habit called stimming! It started soon after birth. As a toddler, I would cross my legs, get really tense and stiff, and rock back and forth. I would do this when I was stressed. This was done, I guess, because of hyposensitivity, which means that I was lacking some sort of feeling I wasn't getting. I'm not 100% sure. I also loved to go under tables, and I don't know why. It was more fun, safe and comfortable – like a hug, I guess.

SHARI:

One of the earliest indicators of Brittany's autism was stimming. Stimming is self-stimulatory behavior – the repetition of physical movements, sounds or repetitive movement of objects common in individuals with developmental disabilities, but most prevalent in people with autistic spectrum disorders. It's considered a way for people with autism to calm and stimulate themselves.

Therapists view this behavior as a protective response to being overly sensitive to stimuli, where the individual blocks less-predictable environmental stimuli. Another theory is that stimming is a way to relieve anxiety and other emotions. Common stimming behaviors (sometimes called "stims") include hand flapping, rocking, head banging, repeating noises or words, snapping fingers, etc. Stimming is almost always a symptom of autism.

From birth, Brittany would stim in different situations: as she tried to breastfeed, while in the crib or in her high chair. She usually would start by stiffening all of her muscles in a sort of full-body flex. She would do that over and over, sometimes holding it for a while.

For about three years from the time she was around 3, she would move her fingers in a sort of flexing, waving motion. This is often called "counting."

Then there was the rocking. It seemed like she was always rocking. She could be sitting on her bed, reading a book or in her car seat. It would start out casual, but with Brittany there was a definite beginning, middle and end – a sort of cycle that had to play out. Or else. There was a pattern that only she was aware of, but if we tried to stop her or interrupted her pattern, she would totally lose it. She had to finish the rocking cycle.

TRAVEL

BRITTANY:

> Whenever we traveled, I wanted something familiar with me. I always took my favorite Beanie Babies. Looking at photos of me when I was little, I can see that I always had those toys with me, especially on airplanes. Whenever we would fly, my OCD got really bad. I had a thing where I always wanted my seatbelt on really, really tight. I didn't like it loose at all; it really bothered me.

SHARI:

It was really difficult to go anywhere out of the house. In those early years before Brittany was diagnosed, we didn't realize how upsetting it was for her to leave the safe surroundings of her room and her home to go, well, pretty much anywhere – in the car, out shopping, visiting friends, etc. I had to fight to strap her into her car seat or her stroller.

When I visited my family with her in Arizona, my brother-in-law Michael decided that he was going to "break her" of being upset around them by taking her into a room and playing with her until she stopped crying. He was pretty confident that he could outwait her. Two hours later, Michael came out of the room and said he needed a drink. She broke him.

Flying was a nightmare. The noise, lights and general chaos were extremely overwhelming for Brittany, and she would pretty much cry nonstop. This didn't make us too popular with the other passengers. We were flying on United Airlines one time when a flight attendant took it on herself to scold Brittany for being such a "bad little child." She never asked if we were OK, never tried to talk to me first. I was beyond upset at her utter lack of sympathy or professionalism and mortified that she singled us out like that.

FIXATIONS

BRITTANY:

> *If you have a kid who likes to wander off like I did, KEEP AN EYE ON THEM!!! We're wandering away because A) we're bored, B) we see something we like, or C) we want to explore.*

SHARI:

I found out later about the tendency autistic children have for developing fixations on certain things. For Brittany, it was balloons – dear God, the balloons! In stores, floating randomly outside, anywhere there was a balloon, Brittany was drawn to it like a magnet. We dreaded going to children's parties. If she brought a balloon home, she would never let it out of her sight. Eventually – when it really needed to be thrown out – we had to wait until she was asleep, sneak it out of her room and hide it in the garbage so she didn't know where it went.

Children with autism also can be "runners," where they slip out of sight in a split second. Protecting a child on the autism spectrum from "running" is, for a parent, a vital safety concern and can be a matter of life and death.

It wasn't long before we realized that Brittany was a runner. She would run away really fast for no apparent reason. A lot of times, it was to chase a balloon. One minute she would be right there with us, the next minute she would disappear.

It's funny, for a kid who hated to leave home and travel, she had no problem taking off alone on a whim when she was little... without any concept of how long she was gone... or if it was safe or scary... or who was around her and what was going on. Nothing.

Something would catch her eye, and off she went. Frantic and with local law enforcement on the phone listening as I described what she was wearing, someone in the search party (friends and family) would yell, "She's on the beach." And there she was, building a sandcastle, not a care in the world, looking at us with no idea what the commotion was about.

When Brittany was 10 years old, I was shopping at one of those giant warehouse costume and decorations stores with both kids at Halloween time. I was no amateur at this point; I knew that she had a tendency to wander off. I kept an eye on her at all times, certain I could handle it.

I turned slightly away from her, lifted my arms to take a princess costume she had been pointing at off the rack, turned back to show it to her and – boom – she was gone! I grabbed the first employee I saw and screamed at her to shut the front doors and back entrances, that my young autistic child was on the loose, lost somewhere in their cavernous store.

Matthew and I spent the next 30 minutes running around screaming her name, looking in and under and around everything in that store for Brittany. Thirty minutes is an eternity when your child disappears.

I eventually ended up calling the police. We had searched the entire store and found nothing. They arrived to get a description from me and start a search when, all of the sudden, she crawled out from under a large pile of costumes at the back of the store. After the first few seconds of sheer relief, I demanded to know why she didn't answer me. I knew that she must have heard me and all of the store employees calling her name for the past 30 minutes.

She had no answer, no idea that she had created such an incident, no idea of the time she had spent cozy under that pile of costumes, no idea that we were freaking out not knowing where she was or if she was OK.

There I was, in my own personal Halloween nightmare, surrounded by costumes, scary decor, irritated store employees and police officers. Brittany had wandered before – lots of times, in fact. But I remember this one incident so clearly. My marriage was falling apart, I felt guilty, angry and scared out of my frickin' mind. Everything was piling on and working together to create one giant breakdown, which I felt I was having right there in the middle of Halloween Central.

OBSESSIVE BEHAVIORS

BRITTANY:

Sometimes obsessions can be good, but make sure if your kid has obsessions that she doesn't take them too far. Many times, they'll be really obscure obsessions. Just go with it. But if it's unhealthy or getting in the way of school or other important things, rein it in.

My OCD is all over the place. I've been obsessed with balloons since I was 1; knew all about different dog breeds before we got our dog Max; knew random facts; liked werewolves, Marvel superheroes and comics; and collected art, coins, guitar picks, shiny rocks and other weird stuff I found on the ground.

My OCD also manifests with other weird stuff, like how I wear my clothes and deal with textures, smells and sounds. For instance, I mostly just wear 100% cotton. I hate scratchy clothes or materials that make sounds or irritate me in some way. I remember back in the '90s, mom got me a new shirt that was popular back then. The fabric was all crinkly, like an accordion, in blue and pink tie dye. I hardly ever wore it because the feel of the pleats and the rustling sound bothered me. All I want is to be comfortable in practical clothes that don't bother me all day.

Then there were my shoes. When I was in elementary school, I liked them tied really tight. And I mean really, really tight. When my parents tied them for me, I kept saying, "Tighter!" They would lecture me about wearing my shoes too tight, but I had to have it that way.

While growing up, we had a red table in our playroom that we used for our Legos. I hated the texture of that table and the sound it made when you ran your hand over it. It still gives me the shivers thinking about it. I also hated cutting boards. The sound they made when you washed them really bothered me and, when I was supposed to do dishes, I wouldn't do those.

Strong smells have always bothered me too. I can't walk into an Abercrombie in the mall or any other place with lots of candles and scents because the smell is super intense and really bothers me.

When I was a kid, I hated the sound of a flushing toilet. I don't know why, I just did. For a while I wouldn't flush... until my parents started getting mad at me for that. Even then, I would stretch out as much as I could, flush the toilet, then sprint out of the bathroom every time.

SHARI:
A number of psychological disorders – including obsessive-compulsive disorder (OCD) – frequently co-occur with autism. As a professional would explain it, OCD is characterized by obsessions or compulsions or both. Obsessions are recurrent and persistent thoughts that are both intrusive and unwanted. They cause significant distress, and ignoring them can be difficult.

Individuals with obsessions often try to manage the discomfort by performing a particular action; this is the "compulsive" part of the disorder. Compulsions are time-consuming, repetitive behaviors that an individual feels driven to perform in response to an obsessive thought or feeling.

Brittany started exhibiting symptoms of OCD in 5th grade, when Terry and I started having marital problems. We were fighting a lot and finally told the kids that we were thinking of getting a divorce. That's when the hair pulling started.

Hair pulling is an OCD-related issue called Trichotillomania – a form of self-stimulation and control that's common in autistic,, Asperger and OCD children. Brittany would pull her eyelashes and eyebrows out one by one. Later, when she ran out of hair on her face, she would pull hairs from her head, one by one. She said that the sensation helped her feel in control.

The trauma of our pending divorce apparently was the final push for her. When her anxiety levels would get worse, the hair pulling would get worse.

Unfortunately, while she has better times here and there, the hair pulling never really stopped; she still struggles with it. I've tried everything I know to help her – hypnosis, counseling, group therapy. Nothing works. At some point, she must want to stop. She is more self-aware now but still can't really control it.

As she got older, she learned how to apply makeup to conceal her lack of eyebrows so she doesn't stand out so much. And she pulls the hair on her head out from a small spot on the back of her head that she can cover by brushing the rest over it. No one else sees it, but I know, and it still bothers me. They say it's a virtually impossible habit to break, just a part of being obsessive-compulsive, but I don't stop trying to find ways to help her with it.

I recently bought her a toy at the Puzzle Store that was like iridescent play putty with a light inside. It was probably meant to be used as a stress ball type of thing, but I thought it might keep her hands busy and her mind distracted from the pulling.

I was willing to try anything that made sense to me, especially with the onset of hair pulling. I was always in search of the best, the newest and the groundbreaking for my daughter to help her overcome what I thought of as a phase with the hair pulling. We tried hypnosis, which ended up being a waste. Good old-fashioned bribery – new clothes, money, you name it – didn't work either. I constantly bought things for Brittany to play with to keep her hands busy, like the glowing putty toy from the Puzzle Store. But the bottom line is that you just can't stop OCD. It comes down to the person gaining self-awareness and understanding in order to gain control over the things she's compelled to do.

UNDERSTANDING WHAT MAKES US TICK

BRITTANY:

I have to say also that you really need to have a lot of patience and understanding when it comes to dealing with an autistic person.

I sometimes have trouble organizing my time and dealing with being overwhelmed. Like when my sister got married. There were a lot of events going on before the wedding. My dad explained the schedule to me, but I didn't understand. He tried again, and then my brother tried to explain it to me saying the exact same thing. I still didn't get it. Then my sister-in-law explained it (third time's the charm), but she explained it by what outfits I needed to wear – and I finally understood.

And then, of course, I forgot again (it was a complicated schedule), so I texted my dad. He texted me back, but I didn't understand the text message, so I called him, and he started getting angry that I still didn't get it. Then my mom came to the rescue and had him tell her what was going on. She had to explain to him that sometimes I just don't get certain things.

Then she came up with a really cool idea to help me. You can repeat some things all you want, but a lot of times I still won't get it. My mom has learned a lot of patience with me and ways to help me get organized and remember stuff like this.

For example, with this super-complicated wedding weekend that was stressing me out, mom saw that I was struggling with understanding and remembering which outfit I had to wear to the different events. She came up with the idea of using masking tape to label each piece of clothing for the event it was intended for. She did it for everything – shoes, tops, jewelry – all of it. It worked! I didn't have to worry about wearing the wrong thing, and the weekend was saved.

The simple masking tape fix worked great. I think because it was simple. I couldn't understand the technical way in which my dad and brother were explaining it. It may be different for other people.

What I'm trying to say, though, is that if you're trying to do a task, explain something or whatever to an autistic person, and they don't seem like they're getting it, try doing it a different way. Odds are that they do get it, it's just that they don't understand the way you're explaining it. So please be patient and try to understand that when you get frustrated, we get frustrated and upset too. This isn't the first time it's happened to me, either.

It's really embarrassing and frustrating when this happens with friends. I would nod with a blank stare and say that I understood when I really didn't because I felt bad. What I SHOULD have done was ask them to explain it again – but differently maybe, in a more visual way. Sometimes it can be a simple thing, but to us it's complicated! So please just be calm and patient, and try to understand.

SHARI:

When Brittany was in middle school, we decided to have a special kind of MRI (brain mapping) done on her brain. Her pediatrician recommended it, but it was a unique procedure at that time, and we had to look around a bit before finding a neurologist in Santa Monica who was able to perform it on Brittany.

What was interesting about mapping her brain was seeing the areas that were "hot" and "cold," or what was being used more and used less. The frontal lobe was hot, which they say explains the OCD. It also confirmed that she was reading a lot (voraciously, in fact!). The memorization part of her brain was hot as well. The part of the brain that deals with math was cold, though, which didn't surprise us one bit. We had a literal map to our daughter's brain that gave us insight and guidance for how to support her best. It told us a lot about why she thinks the way she thinks.

Brain mapping is an effective way to see into your child's brain and focus on her strengths and weaknesses – and what you need to focus on to help her. I highly recommend doing it if you're able to. You need as much insight into how your child's brain works as you can get.

As parents, our emotions can take over and drive everything we do. The brain-mapping MRI helped me pull back and look at things more critically, removing emotion from the equation. Once I could clinically understand these things about my daughter's brain and how it was working or not working, I could approach the next steps in a way that really gave her the help and support she needed.

TIME MANAGEMENT

BRITTANY:

There are a lot more things you should know about me:

1. *I suck at sarcasm, jokes and things along that line. Why? Because if I can't hear the obvious pitch change*

in someone's voice or see that they are clearly not serious, then I will think that they are telling the truth and being straight with me. I'm not gullible, I just have a hard time reading subtle things like that.

It's not just me. There's this girl I know who has Asperger's and, when we play Apples to Apples, she takes things very literally. It's hard and not fun when someone is purposefully trolling you. It's upsetting. Watch out for this – it might lead to being bullied because other kids think it's fun to mess with you.

2. *It takes me a bit to grasp some concepts so, if it needs to be repeated, please don't get frustrated. It just takes a bit to register what you're trying to explain. Some (most, I think) children who are autistic are visual learners. Visuals help a lot!*

3. *I can't dance very well on beat. I'm always a second behind in choreographed dancing.*

4. *I can't stand certain fabrics! Take care when you buy clothes for your autistic child – make sure they'll actually wear them first. Most of the time it's just about comfort. Fabrics such as wool, tight, thin shirts or anything itchy are not good. (Children with autism often have sensitive skin.)*

5. *Sounds! We have sensitive hearing, so be aware of what's going on around you. If your child is covering her ears or cries a lot as a baby, it might be because it's just so darn loud, or a certain noise is bugging her.*

SHARI:

You want to make sure that your child understands the concept of time. Brittany didn't. She has always struggled with managing her time and still does at the age of 21. When she's in school, she's OK because she's on a regimented schedule. She understands that she needs to be certain places at certain times. Homework has specific due dates. And she is able to plan her study time by using that information in order to get everything done. School offers a much more regimented atmosphere that enables her to manage her time much better than elsewhere.

It's when Brittany's not in school that she loses touch. She'll come home on break and totally lose all connection with managing her own schedule or understanding how it affects others. Whereas she knows to let a professor know she's missing class or is having a friend pick up homework for her, when she's at home, she won't think about picking up the phone and telling her family or friends that she's going to a movie, how long she'll be out running errands or when to expect her back.

Here's a peek into a typical time-management fiasco, á la Brittany: One Friday night during the summer, when Brittany was home from college, I was out with a friend and called the house at 5:00 p.m. to check on her. She didn't answer. I tried again at 5:30. Still no answer. I called again at 6:00 and, at this point, was starting to get a little stressed out because I hadn't heard back. This was a 20-something girl with a fully functioning smartphone. Parents, you know as well as I do that kids with smartphones are NEVER more than one millisecond away from calling or texting at will, no matter where they are or what they're doing. I'm no rookie; therefore, I stressed.

She had a job that summer working at a local doctor's office, so I called the office to find out if she was working late that night. The service told me the doctor was on vacation, so I knew she wasn't there.

I was starting to get really worried. I imagined the worst, was texting her nonstop, totally freaking out and started imagining worst-case scenarios with car accidents and her lying in a ditch somewhere.

Finally, around 7:30 that evening, she called. I was literally about to call the police, and she tells me, very nonchalantly, that she decided to go to the movies. I lost it! I was so upset with her. How could she do this? How could she make me worry so much? How could she be so thoughtless?

Looking back, this is just one of A LOT of incidents where she had no concept of time or the consequences of how what she did with her time affected the lives of those around her. These thoughts just never cross her mind.

This incident was the last in a long line for me. I had reached my limit for what I could tolerate and drew a line that night. We had a really long discussion where I tried to help her understand how hard this was on me. I had pictured her kidnapped, lying dead somewhere, who knows what. I had run myself through the ringer worrying about her.

I told her she was old enough to understand and take responsibility and, while she was living with me, she MUST be more accountable with her time, learn to check in with me and acknowledge how her actions affect all of us around her who love and care for her. I just couldn't go through that over and over anymore.

At first, she was mystified by how I felt. She had no clue that anyone felt that way, that others worried about her or that her actions would affect so many people.

This may sound like too much, but my advice to other parents who deal with the same thing is to create an agreement and have it in writing – a "contract" that you both sign stating the things that you both need, like checking in with each other or answering calls. And have penalties in place that reinforce their desire to stick to it.

Honestly, I think this would work great for all teenagers, not just autistic kids. For teens and young adults on the autism spectrum scale, however, I believe it's essential that we help them understand what their actions should be and what the consequences of their actions are for themselves and for the people around them.

Whatever you do, don't coddle them. You have to be realistic. The world isn't perfect. No one is perfect. You have to know when to push and when to back off. Believe me, I've been guilty of trying to make Brittany's life easier. It's natural to want to protect her. But we're not doing autistic children any favors by leading them down a path lined with bubble wrap. They need these skills to survive and thrive without us. And isn't that the ultimate goal?

MEDICATION

BRITTANY:

Mom would ask me sometimes when I was a kid how the medications I was taking were helping. I didn't really notice or know how to answer. Once, in high school, I accidentally took an extra pill that made me feel super drowsy during class. That's really all I remember "feeling" when taking medications.

You know, when you're taking your medication and it works right, everything feels good. So you think you don't need it anymore. Then you stop taking it. And the next thing you know, your mom is saying, "Wait a minute, Brittany, you're talking way too fast. Are you taking your meds?" That's what I mean, I never notice a difference, but it's my mom or brother or dad who would notice and tell me.

In college, sometimes I would ask my roommates if they noticed a difference, since they're the ones seeing me and talking to me, right? They should know!

SHARI:

It was Brittany's hair pulling that finally pushed me to look into how certain medications could be used to deal with some of her symptoms. With the help of her doctors, we tried different kinds, but it's hard to get things right when you're dealing with a developing teenager. We started with Dr. Michael Goldberg, a pediatrician who specialized in autism. At the time, he had a theory that autism was an autoimmune disease. A lot of doctors in the industry didn't agree with him back then. His ideas were considered too "out there" by traditional doctors. He was the kind of person you either loved or hated.

I liked him. I was impressed with his books and presentations and was willing to give him a try. At that point, Brittany began receiving gamma globulin injections to boost her body's autoimmunity systems. She started supplementing with Vitamin C, Iron, CoQ10 and Omega fish oils. We stopped the injections, but she still takes the supplements to this day, and we feel that they've made a big difference in her energy, ability to focus and general well-being.

Over the years, other pediatricians and therapists prescribed other medications. Each child is vastly different, so I won't tell you exactly what we've done. It's important that you have your own child extensively evaluated so that the doctor can make informed decisions about what's best. And you should do your own due diligence when choosing the doctors who will be prescribing for your child. Don't just look at Yelp reviews. Talk to local support groups in the community. Ask for referrals from doctors you trust. Read up on their published articles, any books they've written, lectures given, affiliations, etc.

I will advise, though, that with medications, it's really important that you stay on top of watching your child and knowing what's going on with her. It's common for kids to think they know best. (Shocking, right?) They'll take the medication, have good days and feel better, then stop taking it because they believe they don't need the meds anymore. Brittany would come home from college in the summer, have good days and stop taking her meds. Then she'd have a downswing and not understand what was wrong.

If you're going to commit to using medication as part of your child's therapy, then you've got to get in sync with her moods and the nonverbal signals she's constantly sending. Once you find the medications that work, don't sit back and think you're done. As children grow, their body chemistry changes, and the medications have to be adjusted along with it. You have to be able to recognize what your child needs and when she needs it. She may not realize what's going on, so it's our job as parents to know.

A SPECIAL CONNECTION WITH ANIMALS

BRITTANY:

Some of my earliest memories with animals were these two cute little Bichons at the beach named Missy and Ariel. They were always with this little old lady with blue hair. I loved them. I always wanted to have a dog of my own, but when I was little I had to settle for stuffed animals and Littlest Pet Shop toys. Getting Max, my Bichon Frise, was a total surprise.

When I was in 7th grade, mom and I volunteered at the school's charity fashion show. Max, believe it or not, was one of the auction items. They let me pet and play with him, and I fell in love. I spent my whole time before the show with him. I didn't know he was a boy, so I took a picture with him and called him Sugar.

Dad was there for the event, so I showed him the picture and didn't think anything more of it. Pretty soon, Max was on the runway and being auctioned off. I was totally shocked when I saw dad raise his hand during the auction to bid. Every time my dad raised his hand, I couldn't believe it. I was so emotional. I was crying – I just couldn't believe it was happening.

We had just recently moved, were renting where we lived and weren't supposed to have dogs. I wondered what was going through dad's head. I think he just saw how much I wanted him and was so enamored with him. I told dad that "Sugar" was one of a kind, and I was so in love with him. The auction finally ended up at around $800 and... boom!... the dog was mine!

Mom had no idea what was going on. She was volunteering somewhere else during the program and not paying attention to what was going on up on the runway. Then someone asked her, "Did you know your ex-husband just bought a puppy?" She sort of freaked. We had no supplies, no idea what to do. But she knew with one look that this was the dog for me. This was what I needed. I was in love, remember?

So I fashioned a toy out of a lanyard at home. My mom found a trainer who worked with him and me at the same time. We also took an obedience training course in the park with other dogs. It was amazing!

I was the main one who trained and worked with Max. I think that having him to teach was really good for me. I don't think he was intended to be a therapy thing, but it ended up that way. He's definitely a stress reliever for me. When he's with me, he likes to cuddle, be petted and loves attention. He's been great for helping me stay calm and connected. I don't know if my parents meant for that all to happen, but it definitely worked out that way.

When I left for college, he was pretty depressed and mopey. Mom brings him down to visit me sometimes, which is great. Having Max in my life has definitely been amazing. He's my big ball of sunshine, and we have a very special bond.

SHARI:
Study after study has shown that interacting with animals brings many benefits to children with autism. Research states that children with a family pet tend to have greater social skills. It's also been shown that anxiety, mood swings and depression greatly improve after even short play periods of one-on-one time with an animal.

This has been proven to such an extent that a number of Autism Speaks Community Grants are offered around the nation to support equine-therapy programs for children with autism. Animals provide unconditional nonjudgmental love and companionship – something that everyone can benefit from, but most of all children struggling with some of the harsher effects of autism.

When people ask me when I realized that Brittany had a special connection with animals, I always think back to a moment when she was 3 years old and we were visiting friends on their ranch in Ojai, California. After a tour of the farm, we settled inside to chat for a while, not realizing that Brittany had wandered off.

A bit later, after a panicked search inside and out, we found her in the middle of the horse paddock holding a polo mallet, wearing a jockey hat and having an intense discussion with the horses that surrounded her. It looked like she was holding court, jabbering away with no fear or indication that she was doing anything but having a serious, intelligent discussion with her new friends.

The horses didn't seem to mind either, having drawn up into a circle around her. I can only imagine what they were thinking as they listened to this little munchkin with her silly hat and polo mallet talking and talking.

At the time, I was more focused on coaxing her out of the paddock without spooking the horses, but looking back I realize that was when I first noticed the connection Brittany had with animals. A seed was planted in my mind, you could say, and from then on we tried to find ways to give her more opportunities to interact with animals.

Life was crazy in those early years, and then the divorce made things more difficult, but it was inevitable that we finally ended up with a dog of our own – although the way we got Max is pretty unconventional.

BRITTANY:

> Horses have been a special part of my life. Taking care of horses is a lot more difficult than taking care of a dog. There's a lot more that goes into it: brushing their manes and tails, caring for their hooves, getting dirt out of their shoes, brushing, feeding, exercising, etc. Having a horse teaches a lot of responsibility.
>
> I showed up at the stables on my 16th birthday, and there was a HAPPY BIRTHDAY sign over the stall of my favorite horse, Cooper! I was so surprised. Cooper and I rode on the high school equestrian team for about four years.
>
> It was great, but there also were times when I would get frustrated. My OCD acted up, and I was really picky about my uniform fitting just right and super fierce about the competition. I would get really moody and snap at my mom a lot before events because I was so stressed and competitive. Mom put up with a lot.
>
> Part of the stress, and I don't know if it had anything to do with the autism, was that I felt like I was so much slower than everyone. When I did a showing, there was a lot of memorization. For instance, they would show me a blueprint of the area and tell me to go to area 1, then 3, then 5, then 7, etc. I needed to memorize the course almost instantly, and it was really hard for me.
>
> My trainer would go over it with me a lot of times and make sure I got it. This was really important because,

if you hesitate when jumping, the horse will balk or duck. So you can't show any hesitation. All you have to do is be confident of where to go next.

I loved it, but there were a lot of times when I was very frustrated with the memorization. I would threaten to quit, but I never did; I adored horses too much.

Forgetting a course was really embarrassing, and I did that in one show. I mean, you had to create a mental map of the course in your head and where to go when. It's not like the horse has a GPS. He's depending on me to know where to go and when to go, when to turn around and when to jump. I think when I forgot which way to go was the only time I threatened to quit. Thank goodness that wasn't typical, though, and most of my training and competition was better than that.

I also was really obsessed with making sure that I wasn't given any special allowances just because I am autistic. If the judges offered to make special allowances for me, I didn't want it! In fact, I didn't even want them to know. If you tell people you're autistic, then they start treating you differently. They look at you differently. If horseback riding ever had an option that let me get around the memorization, I wouldn't have wanted that sort of handicap or way to get around it.

When you're doing a sport, you're training and competing against other kids. I wanted to be judged the same way as everyone else – in the ring and out of the ring. I have all these ribbons in my room. I never won first, but I did place second or third sometimes, competing against other kids who were really good. I beat them without special considerations, and it felt even better coming out on top.

SHARI:

A few years after the divorce, we started Brittany with riding lessons. I found a local place that was highly recommended, and we started with just leasing a horse. Money was tight, and I wasn't sure how this would all play out, but I knew she really connected with animals and thought this would be a great way to encourage and support her.

I was right. She really got into it during her middle school years, but it was in high school when her love deepened even more, and she joined the equestrian club. This was yet another breakthrough. She was able to compete with other schools, be part of a team and be in a space where she belonged. Horseback riding taught her a lot about life, health, discipline, competition, focus and a lot of things that traditional sports do, but that she'd never had access to before. It was worth every cent.

There's something about watching an autistic child with animals, especially horses. It was amazing, even beautiful, to watch her interact and communicate with the horses. Her first horse was leased, and then we bought her a horse, Cooper, for her 16th birthday. It was the best time of her life, and it was the greatest for a parent to see her self-esteem improve, her muscles and posture improve with the exercise and even her physical fitness go up a notch.

Low muscle tone is often a problem for kids with autism. They tend to slump a lot when sitting, as their core isn't very strong. Sports are difficult because their muscles aren't as strong or resilient as those of their peers. Riding horses brought the unexpected bonus of helping Brittany develop her core muscle strength. The improvement was amazing.

This new level of physical fitness also made a difference in her academic performance. She wasn't exhausted or slumping in her desk during class anymore. She was able to concentrate and focus. Plus, that connection between her and her horse, Cooper, was a beautiful thing to see. It was very sad when we had to sell him when she went off to college, but she couldn't spend the time with him that she needed to at that point.

I highly recommend horse therapy or finding a stable where your child can interact with horses in some way. It's an amazing tool for self-esteem, exercise, focus and so much more. When it comes to exercise and sports, too, it's a much better alternative than traditional team sports. Kids on the autism spectrum have trouble with team sports, as it's really difficult for them to handle the group interaction.

It doesn't have to be horseback riding. Individual sports such as golf and tennis are better suited for autistic children as well. We had Brittany try playing golf for a while, too. She had a funny bow-legged stance because her legs were so weak, but she would step up there and manage to hit the ball. She played for a few years with her father and brother until she moved on to something else.

Take it from me... horse therapy is phenomenal for special-needs kids. It builds confidence, communication skills, strength and resilience. There's a special bond between the kid and the horse – the touch, the care, the connection with another living being.

SELF-ESTEEM

BRITTANY:

Horseback riding and drawing helped me feel really good about myself. When I would get really stressed – but would do well jumping or drawing – I felt successful and good. Self-esteem is really important. Doing something well, creating things with your hands, it all helps a kid feel like they are good at something. This is important for them to feel good about themselves.

Mom always told me that I could do anything, that "can't" wasn't in our vocabulary. My parents had me try a lot of sports and different things growing up. If I didn't like them, fine, but they insisted that I try.

It was a good thing, though. For instance, I didn't know I liked to draw until later on. I wasn't sure I wanted to draw for a while, but my parents saw the potential and kept at it. It's like dipping your toe in a pool. Keep testing the waters, keep trying and eventually, if they figure out they like it, they'll jump right in.

If your kid has a hobby she really likes, even if it's something weird or strange, if it makes her feel good, I don't see why she shouldn't do it. You never know what's out there.

I know this guy who makes 3D paper models for a company. It's a thing! He always loved Star Wars and origami and stuff as a kid, and now he has a great job doing what he loves. There's something out there for everyone. If you want to help your kid with self-esteem, help him explore and find his passion, and then support him. It's worth it!

SHARI:

It's important when your child is young to help her explore, try new things and always be on the lookout for that thing that catches her attention and ignites her passion. Children on the autism spectrum stereotypically develop a hyper-focus on things that they enjoy, almost to the degree of an obsession. It's all OK, as long as you help them channel it positively and keep balance in their lives.

This focus, though, can be a lifesaver in so many ways, giving them direction in life, finding something they enjoy and leading them to a place where they feel comfortable and in control.

Try lots of different classes. Read books, and go to museums with hands-on exhibits. Try to figure out what your kid is passionate about, and go with it. No matter if it's writing, art, computers, surfing or robots, you need to support and nurture what she loves doing. Once you see what she's into, find classes, enlist the help of mentors and do all you can to encourage her to join in with other kids who like the same thing.

After the divorce, finances were tight. My ex-husband was withholding alimony payments, and the kids and I were forced to live in a horrible condo for eight months. It was depressing. But the bright spot was that we met a neighbor who had a son with autism in the local high school. As an older high school boy, he had never gone to a dance, never attended a social function. He was only a few years older than my son, high functioning, brilliant, and really into computers and space. Long story short, he now works for NASA. His parents saw his passion and did everything they could to nurture it as he grew up. I knew I wanted the same for Brittany.

It wasn't long before we found one of Brittany's great passions: comic books. After the divorce, when my ex-husband would take the kids on weekends, they would often visit the comic book store. I had no idea at first, but Brittany was hooked. Pretty soon she was wearing T-shirts with superhero logos and collecting massive amounts of comics that she kept under her bed.

Comics became an obsession. It wasn't just the love of the story or the art; comics became a safe place for her. She felt normal when she escaped into that world. Pretty soon, she only read comic books and fantasy novels. It truly became an obsession. To this day, she has thousands of comics and won't let me get rid of them. They're stored in huge bins and, when she comes home from college, she pulls them out and goes through them all – always with great enjoyment.

Remembering how our neighbors across the street supported their son's interests, once I realized that Brittany's passion for comics and animation were more than just a passing trend, I found a local art teacher for her. This was a great move. She really loved the experience, and the teacher and instruction were good for her in many ways. Her instructor, Sheldon Borenstein, was an art professor at Chapman University and San Jose State and gave individual lessons locally, as well. He pushed her to excel. Sometimes her feelings would get hurt or she would get discouraged, but he really supported her and was instrumental in helping her build her portfolio and consider pursuing a degree in animation.

As I wrap up this chapter, I feel compelled to share that of all we've talked about and all you can do for your autistic child, nurturing her self-esteem is one of the most critical. People tend to get bogged down in the details of diagnoses, symptoms, doctors, therapies, medicines, classes, tutors and all of that – so much so that they forget to look at the child and realize that how she feels about herself is of even greater importance.

Nothing breaks your heart like knowing that your child feels that she isn't worthwhile, that she's "broken." She may try something to please you – sports, dance, clubs, etc. – but really not think she's good enough.

When kids are young, you can put them in a tutu or on a soccer field, and they can run around in circles, windmilling their arms and not really accomplishing anything. People call it cute. Once they get older, though, and activities become harder, they reach a point where they can't progress any further, and it will be frustrating. And discouraging. And heartbreaking. Both for them and for you.

When they find their passion in life, they shine. A mother couldn't ask for anything more.

Chapter
3.

Gluten-Free

BRITTANY:

> Now that I'm out on my own, I don't keep an exclusive gluten-free (GF) diet, but it's pretty close. The habits mom instilled are still there, though. I buy organic, high-quality ingredients as much as I can. Because we ate gluten-free growing up, it's become a habit.

> So when I go to places such as Trader Joe's, I buy the same ingredients we did when I was living at home because I know they're good and they're good for me. Sometimes if I eat too much gluten, I can tell the difference in my body and my energy. I've met other students at Chapman who are celiac and gluten-free, which makes it easier to stick to my own GF diet. We

all get into discussions about GF. My roommates like to cook, and we share recipes that are good as is, but we also have GF versions that taste just as good.

Bottom line? My mom taught me how to survive on my own. I've met kids at school who didn't know how to use a gas stove and only ate food that came out of a microwave because their parents didn't think they could handle anything more difficult. And these were kids WITHOUT autism! Parents, you've got to teach your kids how to do laundry, cook, etc., to survive on their own.

SHARI:

Brittany had stomach issues since birth and was constantly in horrible pain. I felt like we consulted with a million doctors about her digestive issues. We started noticing that her stomach seemed unnaturally distended. I had no idea what was going on, so my first thought was that she might have a bowel obstruction.

I took her to UCLA, but they were unable to find anything wrong beyond general constipation. After a few more doctors and many more tests, I was told that she had retentive bowel syndrome, or functional fecal retention, a condition common among autistic children who resist having bowel movements as a means of control. They also diagnosed her with leaky gut syndrome, also common among autistic children.

More than anything, Brittany craved carbs. Her main food groups were Cheez-Its, Goldfish, bagels with butter, tortellini and pasta noodles with butter. She would beg and beg for her favorite dishes until I gave in to her. So I did. I didn't know what else to do, and she was unwilling to eat anything else. It's a vicious circle, though, with carbs. The more you eat, the more you crave. Pretty soon, her cholesterol levels started climbing dramatically. Her blood sugar was all over the place. She suffered from severe acid reflux. Something needed to change.

I didn't know about gluten-free diets, something that could probably have eased her pain, so we lived through the cycles of craving the things that were hurting her most. I didn't know anything about celiac disease or gluten sensitivity. And it wasn't really on the radar yet for doctors, therapists or medical professionals.

Then, when Brittany was 10 years old, my father was diagnosed with celiac disease. Recognizing the same symptoms in her, he asked me if I had tested to see if Brittany was gluten sensitive. I was out of ideas and desperate to try anything. It turned out that she was, so I decided that the kids and I would go gluten-free.

It wasn't easy. It's not like you can tell a 10-year-old that she suddenly can't have any of her favorite foods anymore. So I took the "out of sight, out of mind" approach. Any time Brittany would ask for Cheez-Its, I would tell her the store ran out. Bagels? Nope, sorry, the bakery didn't have any. I made healthy meals – chicken and veggies. She didn't want to eat it at first, and I didn't force it. I just told her that was all we had.

She would eventually get hungry and eat it. She wasn't happy about it, but I became a food tyrant, totally committed to sticking to this new gluten-free regimen for the kids and me. It was a hard transition, but it eventually started to feel normal. And the improvements to her stomach, along with the easing of her pain, told us that we were on the right path.

Then we started seeing Dr. Goldberg. He had some strong thoughts about diet for autistic kids but was more concerned with dairy than gluten. In fact, he sort of pooh-poohed our gluten-free diet, but I told him that it was working, and he had no problem with it.

So we stayed gluten-free, but also cut dairy out of our diets. And he didn't want her eating anything red, like strawberries, which are highly allergenic. At this point, I decided that it was too much to make different meals for everyone. So the whole house followed suit.

By the time Brittany was 13, she was acting better, looking better and feeling better overall. Her stomach problems disappeared, and her energy levels and school performance peaked. In fact, one of her teachers called to talk about Brittany's remarkable transformation and asked what I was doing differently. She said she was more alert in class, had stopped hunching over at her desk and was more outgoing and energetic overall. Finally, something was working!

You know how all the experts tell you that the best way to get kids to try new foods and be more interested in their meals is to have them participate in preparing them? Well, I loved cooking. And I really wanted to involve the kids with gluten-free cooking. But no matter how much I tried, Brittany had no interest whatsoever in how food made it to her plate. Matthew liked to help, and I enjoyed having the kids with me when I was cooking, so I usually ended up dragging Brittany into the kitchen when it was time to prep dinner. She would try to sneak off, but I would drag her right back and do my best to pique her interest. This went on for years until, finally, as she was preparing to head off to college, she asked me to teach her how to cook.

We started out by shopping at different stores to teach her the ins and outs of grocery shopping when trying to maintain a gluten- and dairy-free lifestyle. We went to all different kinds of stores so that whatever there was around her college town, she would know what to do. We started with Trader Joe's, Ralphs and Whole Foods. I showed her different types of almond milk and explained why certain types were better than others. I tried to think about "college foods" such as pastas, sauces, etc. We discussed the differences between gluten vs. non-gluten foods and how eating one or the other would affect her.

We focused on Trader Joe's more than anything, as we figured that would be the main store where she would shop during college. I taught her how to read ingredient labels. I passed on tips for shopping such as checking freshness dates on packages, reaching to the back of the shelf for fresher stock and looking for gluten-free options such as brown rice penne, quinoa rotini and polenta. We had fun shopping, and then we'd come home and cook together. I taught her how to prepare foods such as Brussels sprouts to bring out the best taste. That's a big part of the battle...

learning to make things a certain way to make them more attractive and tasty, especially for picky palates like Brittany's.

We cooked salmon and pasta with sausage and veggies; we explored making our own pasta sauce and salad dressings from scratch. We had fun in the kitchen and now – finally – she's really into it.

She's a big Pinterest foodie – loves taking pictures of what she's making and sharing them online. And now that I have the gluten-free food business, it's so gratifying to see how this part of our journey has helped me see my business as more than just a way to make money; it's a way to help others find the resources and support for people like Brittany or my father so that they can live fuller, richer, pain-free lives.

Chapter
4.

Just Because I'm Autistic Doesn't Mean I'm Stupid!

BRITTANY:

I often had a teacher's aide in my elementary school classes, and I didn't really like it all the time. I didn't like the extra attention I got from the other kids, the questions about who she was and why she was there. I didn't like having to explain it; it made me look different. I was so young, it made me really uncomfortable, and I wasn't able to verbalize how I felt. I think she was there to help me stop or control the stimming, which was distracting to the classroom. Back then, when I really got wound up stimming, it sometimes seemed like I was going into a seizure.

SHARI:

School was a challenge, and that's putting it lightly. I didn't want to put Brittany in a school for autistic children. She was so high-functioning and we'd accomplished so much in those early years that I felt taking her out of mainstream education might work against all the progress we'd made. The kids at the special schools I checked out were all pretty severe cases, and I just didn't feel that my daughter fit in those types of schools. After struggling through a few years of elementary school, I wanted to send her to private school but wasn't in a position to afford the tuition.

Sending your child to school for the first time is hard for most parents, no matter what the circumstances. For me, it was terrifying. Class sizes in our local public schools were huge, and teacher-student ratios were less than desirable.

I started by putting Brittany in a traditional preschool with Matthew. Then she went on to public elementary school. She and Matthew were only a year apart, and Matthew was great about watching out for his little sister.

From the very beginning, Brittany was a voracious reader. She would read in class at the same time the teacher was giving instructions and be able to process both. Teachers would complain that she read too much. Funny – reading "too much?!" It makes me laugh every time I think about it. Still, I tried to teach her that it was rude to read in class when a teacher was instructing, rude to read at the dinner table, but changing this was impossible. Reading was – and is – her love, her escape, her comfort zone.

As she got a little older, we learned that, with testing, you couldn't just give her a piece of paper with a bunch of questions on it. It looked like a big black jumble and was overwhelming to her. Once we understood that, and she was presented with the questions one line at a time, she could process better, and we had a breakthrough.

This is when I requested that the school district provide Brittany with a dedicated aide in the classroom. The school district fought me on that, but luckily I had learned a lot of useful things from the books, phone calls and research, and I knew that the Individuals with Disabilities Education Act (IDEA) provided Brittany with certain rights – rights that schools often aren't very upfront about, as they are expensive or intrusive, or they just don't want to do it. They aren't going to just come out and give you a menu of all the things that you have a right to request, so it's important to do your research and know your rights early on.

With the help of a professional advocate, I finally got the school district to agree to the aide; however, they asked me to sign a non-disclosure agreement saying that I wouldn't tell anyone else they had done this. I was angry and refused to sign their agreement. Where was the fairness in that? Why should I get preferential treatment just because I had the resources to have a professional advocate who knew the law? What about all the other parents who didn't know about this or weren't able to bring in the heavy like I did? No way!

I think the lesson in this is to keep fighting for our kids. People are afraid to fight, but I did, and we ended up getting an aide along with other allowances within Brittany's IEP (Individualized Education Program), all provided by the school district.

The National Education Association website offers some great resources for learning about and understanding the Individuals with Disabilities Education Act. See the Resources section for a link to access a series of documents that explain developments in and aspects of IDEA. These briefs, which use a question-and-answer format, offer detailed information important to educators, administrators, parents and others who are interested in serving the educational needs of students with disabilities.

INDIVIDUALIZED EDUCATION PROGRAM (IEP)

IEPs can be intimidating and totally confusing when you first get started, so I've included some online resources in the Resources section at the end of the book that will help you. In a nutshell, if your child receives special education services, he or she must have an Individualized Education Program (IEP).

The Individuals with Disabilities Education Act requires that public schools create an IEP for every child receiving special education services. The IEP is meant to address each child's unique learning issues and includes specific educational goals. It is a legally binding document, and the school must provide everything it promises in the IEP.

The IEP describes how the student learns, how the student best demonstrates that learning and what teachers and service providers should do to help the student learn more effectively. An IEP is meant to ensure that students receive an appropriate placement aren't just placed in special education classrooms or special schools. It's meant to give students with special needs a chance to participate in "normal" school culture and academics as much as possible. In this way, the student is able to have specialized assistance only when such assistance is absolutely necessary and otherwise maintains the freedom to interact with and participate in the activities of his or her more general school peers.

Here's a quick look at what an IEP must include, by law:

- A statement of your child's present level of performance (PLOP) – this is how your child is doing in school now
- Your child's annual educational goals
- Special education support and services that the school will provide to help your child reach goals
- Modifications and accommodations the school will provide to help your child make progress
- Accommodations your child will be allowed when taking standardized tests
- How and when the school will measure your child's progress toward annual goals

- Transition planning that prepares teens for life after high school

Don't think this means that if your child has an IEP that she will be taken out of mainstream classes and placed in special education classrooms. Instead, an IEP ensures that your child is placed where she will do best. When it comes to IEPs, I quickly learned that I need to become the expert for my child.

Meetings with various counselors, teachers, administrators, etc. can be intimidating at first. Everyone will tell you what's best for your child. You need to be able to listen, then respectfully agree or disagree. You're the person with your child 24/7. You know what she needs and, bottom line, you're the one who has the power to make the final call on what's best for your child.

Formal IEP meetings are scheduled once or twice a year, but you generally have the right to request meetings with school representatives, teachers, counselors or anyone else involved whenever you have a need. At first I attended IEP meetings with a professional advocate to help guide me through the process and make sure I wasn't missing anything. Think back to the non-disclosure incident, and you'll understand.

It sounds clinical, but an IEP meeting can actually be a very emotional experience. The educators, school district representatives, counselors and professionals who attend the IEP meeting will be straightforward about what's going on with your child. And it might be hard to hear. We're moms, these are our kids, and it's only natural. That's why I highly recommend that you always take someone, professional or not, to assist you during the process – if only to serve as a buffer when things get emotional and you lose track of the things you want to accomplish.

If you can't handle what people are going to say about your child, you need to have someone with you to act as advocate. You can't let the school district dictate what's best for your child. Brittany's father was rarely able to go to IEP meetings with me, so I relied on friends whom I trusted to help me through the process and be supportive – people I knew would be objective and were on my team.

If you get emotional, and believe me I did, you don't hear what the staff is saying, and it's hard to process everything that's going on. You might be caught up in mental images of a certain incident mentioned, but they'll just keep moving on, and you need someone there to take notes so that you can listen. You can't do both at the same time.

I had input on everything from her physical placement in the classrooms to her schedule to aides and special considerations for testing and classroom work. One of the best parts of the IEP, though, was my ability to have a say in the teachers Brittany was assigned to in middle and high school. I would work with the counselors to look at who her choices were, meet the teachers, sometimes interview them if I felt the need, then choose the ones who I thought would fit Brittany's personality and learning needs best. Every teacher she had was wonderful. What I really hated was that I couldn't do the same for Matthew, who got stuck with some bad ones and really had to suffer through.

At 15, Brittany was able to attend her own IEP meetings. She hated it though, because the school district team would talk about her as if she wasn't there, and she would get pretty upset.

For instance, math was very hard for her. Even with tutors, her brain just isn't wired for math. During the IEP meeting, the teachers and counselors would address the subject as if Brittany wasn't smart and would never be able to handle the subject. During her freshman year in high school, we mentioned something about getting prepared for college, and the school district representatives advised us that Brittany would be better off in community college because she wouldn't be able to handle the stress of traditional schooling. All of this right in front of her.

At that, my awesome child Brittany slapped her hands on the table and said, "Excuse me, I'm sitting right here. Just because I'm autistic doesn't mean I'm stupid!

"My mom taught me that the word 'can't' is not in our vocabulary. I can do anything I want; just because you say I can't does NOT mean it's true. I AM going to a four-year university. A two-year community college is not an option."

Man, I love this kid. And the best part of this confrontation was that it was a big breakthrough for

ME. This was one of the proudest moments I had, right there in that meeting with Brittany. For the past 14 years, I had lived with so much guilt, so much uncertainty, confusion and frustration. Brittany's declaration at the IEP meeting allowed me to finally give myself a break and realize that I must be doing something right. I wanted to stand up and applaud. I couldn't have been more proud!

MIDDLE SCHOOL YEARS

BRITTANY:

Dad was good about helping me with my homework and making me feel accomplished. Even in college, if I had a problem with my homework, I would call my dad, and he would help me. He would read my essays and help me with problems at school, and I always knew I could call him.

SHARI:

Once Brittany entered 6th grade, she needed the help of educational therapists and tutors who understood that she learned differently and also understood how to support that need as she progressed through school. Again, the IEP was a lifesaver for ensuring that the school district provided us with tutors who could help her.

It also was during this time that Terry and I began to have problems in our marriage. We separated, and I decided that a move to a new school district close by would be best for our situation. Moving really took a toll that I didn't understand at the time. I changed

Brittany's environment, moving three times total before we settled into a house in Thousand Oaks. Her autism symptoms got much worse, her OCD flared up, and the hair pulling started.

That's when I started having to go into the school to meet with her teachers and counselors on a more regular basis. I had zero tolerance for bullying. Because of the pulling, Brittany didn't have any eyebrows, few eyelashes and a small bald spot on her head, which exposed her to a lot of teasing.

If someone was bullying Brittany, I was on a mission to make sure it stopped immediately. If it wasn't stopped by the district, I would demand that the bully be moved or expelled or that the situation somehow be taken care of. I wasn't having it. Again, warrior mode.

Middle school was a whole new ballgame, and I became very involved with all of her teachers. I sent emails, called them directly – whatever I had to do to make sure Brittany was on target with her studies and her social interactions. If there were any problems with people bothering her, daydreaming, reading "too much" (again, hilarious!) or just anything, I knew about it, and we were dealing with it in real time.

I was heading straight into a divorce. We'd moved out of the only home my kids had ever known, and knowing that this was harder on Brittany than Matthew, I concentrated on helping her adjust. I didn't realize how hard it was on Matthew, too. He also had left his friends, his life on the beach, school and sports, plus he was adjusting to a total lifestyle change.

Even though he was only a year older than Brittany, Matthew was a natural at taking care of her – sometimes taking on the roles of father, mentor or teacher to her, as well. I often had to tell him to stop and just be a brother. Enjoy being a kid. I think sometimes siblings naturally take on these roles and, as parents, you should watch to make sure they get to just be brothers and sisters.

After the divorce, I took advantage of free or low-cost programs in the community. I found the Tri-Counties Regional Center, a nonprofit organization in California that provides lifelong services and support for people with developmental disabilities. (Again, this is where research pays off!) I took advantage of their respite services, where they paid for a babysitter for a certain number of hours per week so I could get out, shop, exercise and have a small bit of a break.

During this time, Matthew played basketball at the local teen center. Brittany had a hard time with physical activities because of the decreased muscle-tone issues that many autistic children struggle with, but we found her a fencing class at the same teen center, and she loved it.

I mention this here as proof that you just keep trying new things. Don't ever give up trying to find your child's "fit," thereby relegating him to a life of sitting in his room playing video games and/or reading. There's nothing inherently "wrong" with video games or reading – it's just that you need to prepare your child for independence and, like it or not, that means he needs to get out there and interact with others.

In 8th grade, I took advantage of a new opportunity for Brittany and sent her on the class trip to Washington, DC. I was very lucky that the assistant principal, Mrs. Thomas, and her husband watched over Brittany during that trip. They both loved Brittany and became very attached to her.

The next year, when Brittany moved on to high school, Mrs. Thomas was a godsend, always keeping an eye on her. When she called and told me that she was concerned about Brittany walking in circles during her lunch break and always seeming to be alone, we decided to get her involved with the chorus program. Chorus was a good choice for Brittany. It gave her a new community of friends and kids she could relate to and a place where she felt like she belonged.

During these years, Brittany's love of reading reached new levels. It was a comforting, safe place for her – a way to escape from the move, the divorce and the feelings of losing control in her life. She would lose herself in books about horses, animals, Greek mythology and anything she was interested in. She even told me that she loves the "feel" of a book.

I once bought her a Kindle so that she could download eBooks, because there just wasn't enough room in the house for all the books she wanted. But I found out that she didn't like it so much because she missed the tactile feeling of holding a book, seeing the cover, turning the pages, the whole experience. And I really can't be upset; what parent doesn't want her child to have a love of reading?

While I knew she was a big reader, I don't think I really comprehended how much she read and absorbed information about things she was interested in until we traveled to Spain.

For my children, as a graduation gift from high school, I let them pick a place to travel to, anywhere in the world. Brittany chose Spain. So we went to Spain, and I was amazed at how much she knew about every place we visited. She had read many books and guides and retained it all. One of our guides even mentioned that he'd never been on a tour where a child – although she was around 17 at the time – knew more than he did. When we visited a site that she had read about, it was like having my own personal tour guide.

I asked her how she knew so much about the different places, and she told me that during high school – when other kids would go off campus to Starbucks or Coffee Bean – she would go to the library and read every book there was about art, mythology, horses or whatever subjects she was interested in.

HIGH SCHOOL YEARS

The transition from middle school to high school brought on a whole new set of problems. The kids were even meaner. Brittany was alone all the time. She had a rough time with girls bullying her, and it was a constant battle. Matthew and his friends helped a lot. And I was in warrior mode once again, working to make sure the school protected her, nurtured her and ensured her success at school.

It was very important to me to continue to mainstream Brittany in high school, not exclude her or put her in special education classes. If she had trouble, she was always provided extra help or tutors or whatever she needed.

That said, the biggest mistake I ever made was mainstreaming her in math. While she learned just enough to graduate from high school, it was a constant struggle for her to keep up with her peers. Plus, as a result, we ended up having to get a special waiver for the math credits that she needed to graduate from college.

At one point, we had a math tutor who came every day but, no matter how hard we tried, she wasn't able to catch up. It was like beating our heads against the wall. While I still regret this move, I have to tell myself to let it go, too. She can count money, she can balance her checkbook. It's the daily skills that matter.

COLLEGE

When Brittany was a junior in high school, we started seriously looking at colleges. Talk about a whole new set of worries: sex, drugs, alcohol, roommates, classes, navigating campus, the college social scene!

We had the "sex talk" and the "alcohol and other drugs talk." I was very open and let her know she could talk to me about anything. I wanted to protect her and make sure she knew how to protect herself. The talk about alcohol was especially important because she was on medication and had to be extra careful. An accidental overdose can happen more easily when mixing alcohol with prescriptions, and so we talked about her responsibility and understanding the implications of mixing the two.

As she got closer to declaring her major, it became a constant debate between her love of comics and her love of animals as potential career choices. Would she rather be a veterinarian or major in graphic arts, digital media and animation? Both ideas excited her, both were lifelong interests, both she could see herself doing.

In the end, she chose comics and animation because of the value they brought to her life growing up. Comics made her feel safe, special and in a good place. They were her solace, her security. She wanted to learn how to create comics and animation so that she could give back and help other kids like her feel good when they saw her drawings, just like she had while reading the comics she loved so much.

So, as we planned for college and pondered Brittany's future, we looked for schools with a strong arts program that would allow her to develop her talents and passion in digital media and animation. We lived just north of Los Angeles, and Brittany wanted to attend a school close to home, so we turned our sights to Long Beach, Loyola, Chapman and USC. We knew she would probably do better at a small school where she wouldn't get lost and, to be practical, where the opportunities for scholarships would be more plentiful as well.

You can imagine how nervous I was. Sending a child off to college is huge. Sending an autistic child? I was turned inside out. I was so proud and so scared.

Her father and I helped with her application essays. Mr. Borenstein, her art teacher from her teen years, helped her prepare her folio for applying to the Digital Media Animation program. Her first acceptance came from USC, but it was deferred for a year. Nice, but we honestly were holding out for Chapman.

Now I became a "college warrior" and really worked hard to help Brittany get into the school of her choice with the major she was passionate about. Brittany and I traveled to Chapman University to meet with the dean. We attended three official tours of the campus and just knew it was the perfect place.

Finally, we received notice of Brittany's acceptance to Chapman. I had been traveling for work and was in the middle of a conference in Texas when Brittany called to tell me the good news. I transformed from hard-core CEO to babbling proud mom in a matter of seconds, crying tears of joy right there in front of everyone. I was so thrilled for Brittany. She had worked so hard for this, and we were so proud of her!

Mr. Borenstein, meanwhile, ended up as one of Brittany's professors at Chapman, which was a comfort. He taught foundation art skills as well as drawing the human body, animal bodies, anatomy, etc. He taught her how to draw two- and three-dimensional images, further igniting her passion for animation. She was able to learn about and study her favorite artists, William Turner and Roy Lichtenstein. She would visit home on weekends and talk nonstop all day long about her class. She loved it so much.

But everything certainly wasn't perfect. Brittany faced many challenges at college, more so than your average student. But I did everything I could to support her. I visited the administrative offices and made sure that Brittany and I both signed FERPA documents to waive her privacy rights and grant me access to her grades, teachers and counselors. I made sure that Brittany gave me her passwords for logging in to help keep track of her assignments and marks as each school year progressed.

At Chapman, she was offered support through the disability office in case she needed extra time on testing or tutoring or anything special. We set that up immediately when she started there, and she has used that resource. She had terrible anxiety during her sophomore year, and we were able to work with the office and dean of students to ensure that she had someone to go to and resources to help her. We even made sure she could call me and that our wonder dog, Max, could visit to help get her back on track when she really needed us.

Dorm life was good until the first semester of her sophomore year, when her roommate dropped out because of a death in the family. She was very lonely and had a lot of anxiety during that time. I visited her a lot. It was only a few hours away and, between

Max and me, we helped her understand, cope and overcome those challenges.

College has helped Brittany gain a lot more self-awareness, confidence and general ease with the world around her. She's able to recognize when she's anxious and lets me know when she needs help. When she couldn't come home to me, I would grab Max, jump in the car and go visit her.

Anxiety is one of the most common and most difficult things for kids with autism. Developing the ability to recognize, understand and cope with it has been invaluable for Brittany as she moves forward toward her adult life and learns to stride on her own two feet.

No matter where she ends up or what she ends up doing, knowing that the three of us have built a foundation of support is true comfort for me. Brittany, Matthew and I will face whatever comes, secure in the knowledge that we've created this network for each other. We'll all go through tough times, and we'll all be there for each other... no matter what.

Chapman proved itself as the phenomenal fit for Brittany that we thought it would be and one of the greatest experiences of her life so far. She truly thrived during her time there. She traveled to Italy for a special fine arts program, she studied abroad in the south of France, and she interned at prestigious Southern California companies in the industry.

For her animation fix, she's visited the offices of Disney and Pixar and even attended Comic-Con. She's met so many incredible people, corresponding with artists on social media and creating connections that will support her throughout her professional life.

Throughout high school, when Brittany would struggle to connect with peers or find ways to pursue the things she really liked, I always told her to wait for college. That's the place where you'll find people like you, who understand you, who share the same likes. It got her through high school and helped her look forward to college. And I'm so happy that it all came true.

When Matthew or I visited Brittany at school, we would sometimes attend social or networking functions with her and her peers in the digital arts and animation field. We saw the huge difference in Brittany, as college allowed her to indulge and pursue her passion. She opened up and glowed! She networked the room like a pro and had intelligent conversations with colleagues who spoke her language and shared her passion. She was in a place where people understood her, and she understood them. She was truly in her element.

She's had an incredible four years, and I can't believe that as I write this, she will be graduating next week. This is the girl who was told during her freshman year of high school that she would never make it in a four-year college and that the best she might do was community college. This is the girl who slapped her hands down on that table and said, "Just because I'm autistic doesn't mean I'm stupid!"

She proved them wrong. Not only was she accepted to a prestigious private college, but she also received scholarships that enabled her to graduate with very little debt. She's graduating with a full degree, priceless real-world experience and an education that will carry her through a career and life that she truly loves.

If I could go back and make some changes or do things over again, there are a few I think about often. I would look into taking legal action against the district so that they would provide funding for a private school better equipped to support Brittany. I would have talked to local special education advocates to learn more about the different courses of action that were available to us and what combination might work best for Brittany. I wish I had been more educated about the system back then. I didn't know much, and my support system was small.

For instance, I learned way too late that I could have gone to private schools, been honest about my financial situation and asked about scholarships. I regret not knowing about things like that – or not taking action if I did hear about them. I think Brittany would have been happier in a smaller, more intimate setting.

Another thing I feel strongly about sharing with parents of young autistic children: If one of you can quit working outside the home to be with your child and attend the massive number of appointments with school districts, teachers, doctors, therapists and support groups, then by all means do so. I think it's important to focus primarily on your child if you're able to. I realize that not everyone has the means or opportunity to do this, however, so your next step is to research and join local support groups, and see if local services that provide respite, support and other resources to help you and your child are provided by the government or non-profits.

Chapter

5.

Bullying

BRITTANY:

I despise bullies with a burning passion. I was bullied from 4th grade through high school. Bullying hurts so much. I have had to take so much verbal abuse from people my age that it makes me nauseated.

I don't know why I was such an ideal target for bullies. Did my being bullied have to do with my autism? I don't know. I don't think that all of the kids who bullied me knew I was autistic yet, for some reason, I was the ideal choice. Maybe having autistic characteristics made me more prone to being tormented because I was different.

Ninety-nine percent of the time, it was girls who bullied me. Words cut deeper than the sharpest knife. And bullying doesn't even have to be done with words. I've been teased and made fun of with gestures as well.

The bullying was horrible from 4th grade all the way through high school. There was no physical abuse, although there were close calls. Most times it was verbal and, let me say again, words cut deep. It messes with you psychologically. I started to get paranoid. Not fun! When I look back, I realize that I was teased because of my stimming habit, a hair-pulling disorder that I developed when my parents got divorced AND just for being ME.

Fifth grade is when the bullying REALLY started to get bad. I was called a teacher's pet, and my best friend told someone about my stimming habit, which was supposed to be a secret. She apologized later and gave me a candy cane. Not great.

OK, now in middle school, the bullying REALLY HONEST TO G-D BEGINS. I went to Cabrillo Middle School for two weeks before I moved to Westlake Village. During that time, a blonde girl in my P.E. class made fun of me because I had no eyelashes. I don't understand why! I mean, why are people so mean and cruel!? I know that MAYBE she had a backstory of being picked on herself, so she picked on others, but I think she was just a witch spelled with a "b."

So next we moved on to Colina Middle School. It would have been OK if people weren't such MEANIES! Oh my gosh, talk about stereotypical middle school. The most prominent memory I have of that time is a girl making fun of my sweater because it was from The Gap. Her exact words were, "You shop at The Gap?" Now imagine that, but in a snooty tone by a bitchy girl. Yes, she actually said that... I was picked on by guys more than girls in middle school, and whoever said that "when a guy teases you, it means they like you" needs their head examined ASAP. That's a load of poo.

In 7th grade, when I started to pull my hair out from my head, I was picked on by a guy who would mock me in class with his friends when I looked in their direction... IN FRONT OF EVERYONE. It was so cruel and heartbreaking. Just thinking about it now makes me want to cry.

Eighth grade found me in the same situation, but with a different guy (who shall not be named, even though my mother really wants me to name him). He would mock me by mimicking me. He would tease me saying I ate my hair and tease me about liking another boy in class whom, of course, I didn't. He would be like, "Oh, you eat your hair!" because I would often put my hair in my mouth to get to the strand that I wanted. (Yes, the hair pulling was really bad back then.) What's interesting is that as we moved into high school, he was no longer such a jerk. Sometimes people can change – I guess it just took him TWO YEARS!!

SHARI:

I've always told my kids that they can talk to me about anything – and meant it. No judgments, no overreacting, no drama in the moment. We've always been very open as a family and, honestly, I feel that it helped the kids and me get through the divorce, the move and all the other rough spots over the years.

A lot of the time it felt like the three of us against the world, and I knew that if we didn't have a strong, open line of communication, we might not make it through. So I encouraged Matthew and Brittany every day to share what was going on in their lives. It was easy when they were young; however, as they got older, not so much, but by then it had become routine, which helped.

We talked about day-to-day activities, and we often dug deeper to look at how we felt about what was going on in our lives. In the car or in the kitchen, I always kept a conversation going with Matthew and Brittany – and developed the fine art of asking pointed, detailed questions so that I would get detailed answers. The conversations always included questions such as: Did you make a new friend in chorus today? How did you feel about taking the math test? What did you talk to the girls in equestrian club about?

Don't get me wrong – their answers weren't always easy to hear, and I often had to take a breath and work hard to be calm on the outside when I was really freaking out in my head and chanting, "Oh-my-god-what-am-I-going-to-do-now?" over and over.

So I knew when my kids were happy and when they were sad. I knew when they needed space, and I knew when they needed attention. And I knew when the bullying began in Brittany's life.

Middle school was rough. We had moved and were in a new school system. Brittany had started pulling, so her appearance exposed her to a lot of teasing. I didn't know it then, but Matthew became her protector at school, while I found a whole new world of worry and stress.

BRITTANY:

> The same people who picked on me in middle school were still there in high school. Ain't that just peaches? If they weren't my tormenters anymore, I got new ones – and this time they were girls. In my geometry class, this girl flat out called me weird. I just turned around and had a "What the hell, man!?" expression on my face.
>
> The geometry teacher would hum songs, and I made it a game to guess what they were. It was fun... "My Fair Lady," Phil Collins, etc. That teacher didn't mind, mainly because I was probably one of the only students who gave a crap about his class. I wasn't an A (I got a B) student, but I tried my best.
>
> This one girl was TERRIBLE! I had a confrontation with her and almost lost my self-control as I tried not to punch her and tackle her to the ground in front of the teacher after class. Basically, she didn't like me because I was being myself, I think. In my American

Sign Language class, sophomore year or maybe junior year, this one girl would mock me and tease me about my hair pulling with this other girl across the room.

Senior year was a hell of a lot better. For some reason, people started to grow a Jiminy Cricket on their shoulders. Better late than never, I suppose.

A lot of times, I was bullied because of a habit (stimming) that I think most people with autism have, as well as for just being myself.

So here are some tips on how to deal with bullying – from one autistic kid to another:

WHAT TO DO:

1. *Ignore them. I'm just gonna put it on the list but, honestly, it really doesn't help. Those bullies are nothing if not persistent. Bother, bother, bother, bother, bother, bother, bother.*

2. *Tell your parents. They want to know, and they will help! This is more of a last resort. Ask them for advice, or have them do something (depending on the severity).*

3. *Tell the teacher. It's not tattling if you're being verbally abused numerous times. Schools have a zero tolerance policy, so they take this quite seriously.*

4. *Confront the bully... WITH A COUNSELOR PRESENT! Yes, confronting the bully is a must*

if he or she won't leave you alone. Enough is enough. But have a counselor present to mediate and make sure things run smoothly. I know confronting the bully is scary but, if you want it to stop, it needs to be done.

WHAT NOT TO DO:

1. *Tell your older sibling, and have him defend you. This is not a good option. My older brother did this, and well... the bully got scared. I DON'T KNOW WHAT HE SAID... it was a bad situation.*

2. *Threaten that your older brother (or sister) will kick the bully's ass. I didn't mean it, and I only did this ONCE. Threats are taken very seriously by the schools. Don't do it.*

3. *Fight fire with fire. Don't try to say something witty and insulting back. It doesn't help matters and, if you're not good at it, it will make you look dumb – and that's where bad option 2 came in. I'm terrible at comebacks because I don't make it a thing to verbally hurt people.*

Parents, I know you're going to want to take action if your child is being bullied, especially if he or she is autistic. If they can defend themselves to some degree, advise them first and, if it's still out of hand, then intervene – but DISCREETLY!! If they can't defend themselves because they're too severe in the autism spectrum, then by all means... CHARGE!!!

SHARI:

High school brought on a whole new set of challenges. Matthew and his friends were Brittany's champions and looked out for her as much as they could, but they couldn't be there all the time—in every class and in every situation so there was still a lot of bullying. I know that Matthew and his friends had their little "talks" with boys who were bothering Brittany, but dealing with girls was a whole different matter.

When Brittany was a senior in high school, there was a girl who became fixated on making her life hell. She would make fun of her in class, mock her to her face and physically intimidate her around campus.

When the kids were younger, I usually knew when these kinds of things were happening, but this one snuck up on me. First, Brittany tried to deal with it on her own. Matthew had graduated and wasn't at the school anymore to look after her or let me know when something was up.

And worst of all, because of the Family Educational Rights and Privacy Act (FERPA), her teachers were not permitted to tell me when they noticed the bullying going on, as it would violate the privacy rights of the student who was tormenting her.

To give you a little background, FERPA is a federal privacy law that gives parents protection with regard to their children's education records, such as report cards, transcripts, disciplinary records, contact and family information and class schedules. To protect your child's privacy, the law generally requires schools to ask for written consent before disclosing your child's personally identifiable information to individuals other than you.

In a nutshell, this meant that the school was not permitted to release the information about another student bullying my daughter – all because it would be a violation of the student who was doing the bullying's privacy.

One teacher, thankfully, saw the danger in this policy and called me informally on his own time to bring the situation to my attention. I'm still so grateful to that teacher for having the heart and the courage to do what was right and help protect my daughter.

Brittany had just confessed to me at home that she was deeply depressed and struggling, so much so that I was fearful for her mental and physical well-being. Between that and the phone call from her teacher, I had two choices: break down or warrior up. I chose warrior mode.

I walked into the office the next day and demanded that the counselor immediately schedule a meeting with EVERYONE involved – principals, counselors, teachers, they were all there. I remember sitting down, ready to discuss it all rationally, then breaking down as the enormity of the situation settled in. Brittany had reached such a level of depression that I was more frightened than I had ever been. I let everyone in that meeting know that we had a serious problem on our hands, and they needed to work with me to fix it.

I really had to push to get everyone at the table for that meeting, but I also have to give them credit for taking action once we were there, as they realized the seriousness of the situation. They were there for me. They saw my pain and how upsetting it was. And they realized that Brittany had reached her threshold for dealing with abuse from bullies at school.

The years of pain had been building to this point. Thank goodness she felt able to talk to me and let me know how bad the situation was getting before it led to something irreversible.

That day, we all worked together for Brittany. We created a plan for watching and supporting her. The doctors reviewed and adjusted her medications. We changed her class schedule and took action against the bully, who was eventually expelled. And together we made a difference.

BULLYING OUTSIDE OF SCHOOL

BRITTANY:

One summer, I went to a camp called Camp Hill Top for two weeks. It started out fine. The girls and boys were separated into their own cabins. It was the girls who ended up making my life a living hell. They put gum under my pillow so I would wake up with ants crawling on my bed. They locked me out of the cabin and shunned me. Why? I have no frickin' clue.

The one thing I remember is that I wanted to be left by myself, which is normal for autistic kids. We want some alone time, which isn't so bad, but it just makes us stand out in social situations. I would hide in the pool bathroom sitting on the toilet seat moping until those girls would drag me out by my arms and force me back to the cabin like a prisoner. I now call that place Camp Hell Top. I never went back.

There was another camp I went to every summer during middle and high school where I again had trouble with bullying, but I loved the camp so much that I kept the bullying to myself and didn't tell my mom. It was an all-girls camp and, yes, this meant I had more problems with girls. This one girl HATED me – and I mean really HATED me – for reasons I cannot fathom. I asked her once, and her response was, "I don't know, you're from California, I guess." (The camp was in Wisconsin.) Whoa, back up a sec! That was her reason?! She had issues. I was like some exotic bird they'd only heard of before then: cool but strange.

Sometimes I was bullied by this same girl and her cohorts over the littlest (or not so little) things that meant a lot to me. I would cry my eyes out, and they would sit there smirking. They threatened to flush my pillow and Seal (my stuffed animal) down the toilet. They would call him Catsup instead of Seal and make fun of him. I think it was my OCD that made me upset about the name thing. I don't know!

So be aware that if you send your autistic child to a summer camp with non-autistic children, he or she might get bullied. But you know what? I kept going back to that camp because I looooooooved it, and the bullies put only a small damper on my whole experience. I was determined not to let their bullying keep me from doing what I loved. Plus, what doesn't put you down makes you stronger... Isn't that what they say?

Chapter
6.

Matthew's Story

BRITTANY:

> My brother Matthew and I are really close. I've met
> people who aren't as close with their siblings and don't
> understand why not. We get along so well, always had
> the same interests when we were kids, liked to play
> with a lot of the same toys and stuff. I never really
> thought about it. We were each other's best friend.
> We did a lot of things together. I remember when I
> was supposed to be taking a nap, and I would carry
> my pillows into his room because I wanted to be near
> him.
>
> We were always there for each other. I mean, I knew
> that our parents were there for us, of course, but as

siblings, we have a different bond. It's built on loyalty, I think. I'll always be there for him, supporting him and never losing faith in him. And I know he'll do the same for me.

We still stay in close touch. Even though we live apart, we get together whenever we can. We go to concerts and other events, out to dinner and hang out with friends. If anything happens in our lives, we talk about it. He helps me with real-life situations, and I'm so thankful for him.

MATTHEW:

I was 3 years old when Brittany was diagnosed with autism. My earliest memories are of going to lots of appointments with her. I think they told me it was for her speech; I didn't really know why.

Brittany and I were inseparable back then. We were only 12 months apart, and we did everything together. When I was 5, we were playing in her room, looking out the window and talking about what we saw. I still didn't think that Brittany was different, but I did realize that she wasn't talking like other 4-year-olds were. She would make sounds, just gibberish really, but no speech.

When we were alone, I told her if she was scared to talk, it would be alright to talk just to me... that it was OK if she didn't want to talk yet; she didn't have to talk to anyone she didn't want to. I told her not to worry about it and that when she was ready to talk, she would.

When we were in elementary school together, I still didn't think of Brittany as different. We had a lot of the same friends becuase we were only a year apart. I knew that she had to go to speech class and that she had extra tutors that I didn't have, but I didn't really think about it or wonder why.

I knew that she stimmed with the rocking back and forth. I knew it was different and that other kids didn't do it. Once I asked her why she did it. Did she like how it felt? Did it make her feel good? She told me yes, it made her feel good. It tickled a little bit, but she didn't really know why she did it.

Brittany was the type of girl who wanted to do what everyone else did. She was brave and wanted to be like the boys, wanted to hang out with my friends and me and do what we were doing. When we were younger, all of my friends thought that was cool, so she hung out with us a lot.

She also had a problem with wandering. You really had to keep an eye on Brittany when she was little. She would take off without telling anyone and didn't know that it wasn't OK. I remember mom and dad freaking out all the time. She'd see a balloon and take off after it. Or she would wander out to the beach near where we lived if she saw something from the window that caught her attention. I remember a lot of times mom would be ready to call 911, and then someone would spot Brittany playing on the beach, quietly building sandcastles like nothing was wrong.

Another thing about Brittany that was different was her independence at an early age. She didn't mind not having her parents nearby. The fact is, she was pretty oblivious, which is probably why she constantly wandered off. She didn't understand why it was a big deal.

She had no concept of time, either. She would disappear for long periods and think it was only for a few minutes. She's still poor at managing time. She becomes so focused on something she likes that she'll totally lose track and forget about everything else.

Middle school was when Brittany's differences really started to stand out. At that age, everyone wants to be cool. Kids are starting to mature. Boys are noticing girls, and girls are noticing boys. Brittany was still playing with Beanie Babies and those Littlest Pet Shop toys, but I wanted to play outside and be with the guys and do guy stuff, so we didn't play together as much.

Brittany didn't understand why I didn't play with her as often, or why I didn't want to play with the toys she loved so much anymore. This is when I realized that while I was turning into a teenager, Brittany was still a child at heart. The 12-month span between us seemed to get wider. It seemed like we were years apart.

Soon after we started middle school, mom and dad separated. Brittany's OCD really came out in full force, and she started pulling. She would pull her hair, eyebrows and eyelashes out one at a time until she had no eyelashes or eyebrows.

That's also when the bullying started. Kids would make fun of her because she was a 7th grader who basically acted like a 4th grader. I remember one bully who would walk up to her, rub his eyelashes and make fun of her for not having any. That was when the protective older brother in me really came out. I confronted the boy after school and told him that I never wanted to hear about him doing that to Brittany again, or he and I were going to have a serious problem. He stopped, but he wasn't the last one. This just kept going on and on. There are a lot of bullies out there and, as much as I tried, I couldn't deal with every single one of them.

High school was harder, mainly because the girls were so mean to Brittany, and I couldn't do much about it. It wasn't like middle school when I could threaten the boys, and they would back off. If I even talked to a girl who was bullying Brittany, her parents would get upset that I (a boy!) was threatening their daughter. It didn't matter that their daughter was making fun of a special-needs kid. It was crazy.

Still, Brittany wasn't without her protectors. One of my best friends, Greg, treated Brittany like a little sister. We boys were all pretty big, so between Greg, a few other friends and me, Brittany never lacked for people looking out for her in high school.

It seems like I've always had protective instincts, probably because of Brittany. I remember a petite, awkward girl in middle school who was really quiet and shy. The guys always made fun of her. One day, I heard them at it while I was sitting in class. I turned around and told them to stop. I remember her smiling shyly at me, and we were friends after that.

It's not just special-needs kids I feel protective toward. It's more like the underdog kids. You know, the ones who aren't alphas but need alphas to protect them. I think because I had an autistic sister, I became an aggressive alpha so that I could call out kids who bothered her. Along the way, I became a person who looks out for and protects not only Brittany, but others as well.

People ask me if I resented the extra attention Brittany got as we were growing up. I didn't. And I still don't. Honestly! I always understood that she needed the extra attention, and that was just the way things were. It was natural. Along with the protective instinct, I also seem to have an innate ability to "parent" other children. I remember when I was 7 hearing one of my parents' friends say, "He's going to be a great dad." Who says that about a 7-year-old kid? But I really was that way. It's always been natural for me.

Back when our parents split up and were going through the divorce, it was hard – just like it's hard for any kid. We didn't really talk about it with each other at first. Later, when we were on a ski trip, we started talking about the split. Brittany told me she was fine, that she had "forgotten" all about it and didn't have any feelings about it. I told her that wasn't true, and we argued back and forth.

She really didn't think she had any feelings about it and, looking back now as an adult, that may have been true. Brittany often didn't experience feelings the way we do, or she had trouble recognizing what those feelings were or how to deal with them.

Then there were the times when we would wake up in the middle of the night and hear our parents yelling at each other. Brittany would be crying hysterically. She was easily frightened when she was younger. I would hold her and tell her that everything was going to be OK, that mom and dad were just mad at each other, not us, and that it would be over soon. I would take her back to bed and sit with her until she fell asleep.

When she asked me to explain about dad and why the divorce happened, I asked her if she wanted to know the truth. Then she would change her mind and tell me no, that she wasn't ready. She knew that their divorce had to do with infidelity but was afraid that it also might be about her. She wanted to see if she was alone in the way she was feeling but didn't know how to talk about it or process her feelings. So she waited.

It was later in high school when we finally had a heart-to-heart talk about what happened, and she could understand why. When she was younger, she didn't understand what was going on. It was only later, as she matured, that she was able to voice her perspective on what happened and ask for the information she needed to process it all.

In high school, she had trouble processing all the anxiety and emotions that come with puberty. This is normal for teenagers – just think how much worse it is for kids with autism. When she started pulling her hair and eyelashes, I was able to relate and talk to her about it because we were so close in age. I told her how I would have feelings of aggression and anger and how I dealt with them by slow breathing, writing down how I felt and other methods I'd worked on to help maintain control.

I told her that when she felt like pulling, she should do the same: Think about things such as, "What am I feeling? What can I do besides pulling? Can I squish a ball? Can I take a walk outside?" I don't think it worked because, in the long run, it was just too hard to stop pulling – but at least she talked to me about it.

When it came to social situations, most of the time Brittany would just stay home. She was missing out on all of the experiences kids have. I wanted her to realize that there was a world and life going on outside of her bedroom walls. And I didn't want her to miss it.

I talked her into going to the homecoming dance at our high school. I didn't want her to miss out on that experience. I told her she could go with my friends and me in the rented limo, and she could stay with us the whole time. My friends were always really good about including Brittany and really wanting her to be there with us and help her create good memories during high school.

She rode in the limo, had dinner with us at the restaurant and had fun talking to all of our friends. When we got to the actual dance, though, the noise and loud music were overwhelming for her, so she left early. But she did it. I was so proud of her. I wanted her to be brave, try new experiences and not be afraid to get out there. And she did it.

When her senior prom came around and she didn't have a date, I took her – and we had a blast. She was 17 and finally starting to mature. We were still able to talk about everything, just like we did when we were little kids. So we spent the night talking about boys, drinking alcohol and other things that teens are curious about.

I never held back or babied her. I told her the truth and tried to teach her so she could take care of herself in the future. Later on, when she had her first taste of alcohol, I was with her. I made sure that she understood what it would do to her, how much she could have, etc.

She would tell me that she didn't feel pretty and didn't understand why boys didn't like her. I told her not to worry about it because she was just a little behind – she developed much slower than other girls her age. I also tried to help her again with the pulling by pointing out that not having eyebrows or eyelashes made her look different, and she might want to think about trying to stop.

If there's one thing I know from my life with Brittany, it's that the worst thing you can do to someone with special needs is lie to them. I don't mean that you should be harsh and make them feel horrible, but the truth is always best – eased into conversation and delivered gently.

Brittany needed to hear the truth, and that's what she's always gotten from me. It's helped her gain confidence, understanding and insight so that she can clearly see for herself how she affects everyone and everything around her.

Chapter
7.

Overcoming Social Struggles

BRITTANY:

> I enrolled in the PEERS program at UCLA when I was
> 17, and it was one of the best things I ever did. I wish
> I had done it earlier, as it would have helped me
> socially. My mom always encouraged me to hang out
> with friends, but I didn't really want to. I had my mom,
> my brother and my dog, Max. That was enough. But
> when group interactions happened at school, I could
> see that I should have tried a little harder.
>
> In PEERS, we worked together as a group of boys
> and girls, ages 12-18, who all had different levels of
> functioning. Some were more severe, some were less.
> I was one of the higher-functioning kids in the group.

The instructors would talk about how conversations were like a ping pong game. And how we need to be interested in what others think, like, do, etc. We would pass balls as we talked, which helped us recognize shifts in conversation points. This part was really good for me, as I would hyper-focus on one subject and dominate a conversation.

We also worked on making phone calls. I'm still really bad at that. I call my mom sometimes but don't really make calls much to other people unless I have to. We also worked on things such as eye contact, knowing when a conversation is done, watching for openings to join conversations, etc. Jokes and sarcasm were a big part of learning how to act and interact socially. It's still really hard for me to understand jokes and sarcasm.

Please don't think it was all about joking, though. It was a lot more than that. For instance, here are some more things I learned during the PEERS program:

1. ***DON'T BE A CONVERSATION HOG:*** *I know that this happens when I talk about something I love. I tend to get very excited (and a little loud) and talk only about that. The problem with this is that the other person in the conversation gets bored and uninterested. So I learned to keep track of what I'm saying (it's hard, I'm still working on it!) and make sure that the other person gets a chance to talk. I was taught to stay calm and pass back and forth in the conversation – like ping pong. For example:*

Me: "I'm really into animation and drawing. What about you?"

My friend: "That's cool. I tried drawing when I was younger. Do you watch Studio Ghibi animation?"

Me: "Yeah! But I've yet to see Tototro."

and so on...

2. **COMMON INTERESTS:** When talking to people, be inquisitive, but don't be an interrogator. Ask what they like and then, when you learn something about them, talk about it and go from there. If you meet someone you don't have anything in common with, it's likely that you won't hang out in the future, but that doesn't mean you can't be friendly!

3. **INTERRUPTING:** Don't do it! I had a really tough time with this because I often would think that people were done talking, but I was wrong. Watching for social cues like this was really hard for me. And staying on topic! If the topic is cats, don't start talking about llamas. You can smoothly transition to something you want to talk about, just don't jump into it.

4. **PERSONAL SPACE:** Everyone has an imaginary bubble around them. Basically, if you don't know this person or just met her, don't get all up in her grill! I love hugging people, but I also know my limits. I picture that someone's personal bubble is like if they were holding a giant beach ball in front of them.

5. ***HANG OUT AND GET SOCIAL:*** *It's crucial to hang out and be social. Autistic kids usually want to play by themselves because they get to do things their way. Sadly, we don't always get our way, so learn to play with your siblings and peers, and learn to make suggestions for what you would like to do. It's very good to interact with people and not seal yourself away from the world. Dogs don't count; I know that they're cute and fluffy, but they aren't people.*

6. ***KEEP IN TOUCH:*** *Get comfortable having phone conversations. Call your friends, ask how they're doing and if they want to hang out. I'm still working on this, but I'm getting better.*

7. ***EYE CONTACT:*** *Always look someone in the eye when you talk to them. This may seem normal to most, but it's really hard for autistic kids to do. What seems personal and polite to others is really uncomfortable and sometimes scary for us. I had issues with this when I was younger. It was so intimidating to look someone in the eyes. I figured if I could hear them, why did I have to look at them? Imagine, though, if everyone talked to each other while staring at random objects. Annoying and freaky, right?*

SHARI:

Social challenges and autism are natural companions. Both adults and children with autism struggle to deal naturally with the massive number of social interactions necessary for school, work, home, play, friends and family. Just as they say that every kid with autism is different, the way that they approach and cope with social situations also is different. It's not that they can't learn these skills, but more that they may not want to – or they need specific training and practice to help them figure it all out.

Life to an autistic person is like being set down smack dab in the middle of a complicated game where they're the only one who doesn't know the rules. And autistic people aren't the only ones who struggle with this. I've often heard actors with similar disorders confess that they are most confident and comfortable when working from a script, using it as a guide that tells them what to say and when to say it, instead of having to figure it out for themselves.

For non-autistic children, most social skills are learned by observing and mimicking the people around them as they grow up, as if they're constantly writing and editing a script for life in their heads. Everyone from parents, teachers and family members to friends, shopkeepers and neighbors affects how a child learns to interact in a wide variety of situations.

This style of learning, however, is not enough for autistic children. They need much more than that. Everyday social situations must be broken down, analyzed and practiced in order to learn how to deal with them when they arise again later in life. This is true for everything from buying groceries to saying hi to the neighbor at the mailbox to reacting to an assignment from your teacher to dealing with a playground bully.

The best way to help an autistic child find her way through this big, scary social mess is to help her recognize the need, then provide her with professional help, personal support and a hefty amount of patience to get through each day.

BRITTANY:

A lot of social cues are very subtle, and it's really hard for a person with autism to pick up on those. Things such as jokes, sarcasm and flirting are more topics we worked on during the PEERS program. We talked about and practiced recognizing subtle body language cues or changes in voice pitch that would tell us what's going on.

For instance, I was really bad with sarcasm and jokes when I was younger. I still am, but to a lesser extent. When people were being sarcastic, it took me a long time to figure out that there's not really a change in voice pitch. It made me seem like I took everything literally and that I was gullible. I feel like such a fool in those situations, but I've learned to cope. It just takes lots of practice and listening to understand whether people are being serious or not.

Some people I know are REALLY subtle at sarcasm and, when I found out they weren't serious, I was hurt that they were trolling me throughout the conversation. I've learned not to take it personally, but it's hard.

One thing I wish I was good at is jokes – not the obvious ones, but the ones with subtle gags. My major in college is digital arts, and my professor has this saying for stories: "That's the gag!" It took me at least half of the semester to figure out what a "gag" is. I took the meaning of a gag as "knock knock, who's there," when in reality it's something like when a person is about to sit down, and someone pulls the chair out, and they fall. It's all about subtle differences like that. My first few assignments that revolved around gags didn't turn out so well because I didn't understand the concept of a gag. I felt like an idiot. I finally got it, which was good because we had to show our work to the class and, most of the time, no one got mine (so embarrassing). I'm totally OK with being autistic, but this is one of the few times it's annoying.

If you're a parent, PLEASE explain to your child how sarcasm works. As I grew up, the fact that I took everything literally was what often prompted people to make fun of me.

I have trouble with jokes, too. I tend to get caught up in the details when telling a story, when a joke should be funny and short and to the point. So I've just stopped telling jokes and don't do memes, either. I let the funny come naturally instead of forcing it.

Another challenging social situation is flirting. Talk about something that relies on subtle body language and social cues! Flirting with me is like flirting with a wall... it doesn't work. I don't react to flirting because I don't know when it's happening. This relates to sarcasm because both involve subtle body and facial language. I'm still not good at this. I can tell if a guy is flirting if he is being obvious, of course, which comes across as overconfident and annoying. But the more subtle flirting just goes right over my head.

So I'm stuck between a rock and a hard place. My friends say I'm oblivious, which I can't totally deny, but that's not completely my fault. I JUST CAN'T TELL. I ask my girlfriends how they know if a guy is flirting. Some have given me useful advice, others not so much. I also ask my guy friends, mainly my brother, how they let a girl know that they like her. Let's just say that there's lots to be learned on the art of flirting, mainly through Q&A's like these.

People didn't flirt with me in high school. I was bullied a lot. I always felt very self-conscious and was made fun of for my hair pulling, etc. The lack of flirting was kind of hard for me. I'm very romantic and wanted a boyfriend but never had one. It was hard to watch the other kids flirting and dating.

I remember one Valentine's Day I tried to get all prettied up for school and felt really good about myself. I usually didn't do this. I usually dressed more casual, but I felt the most physically insecure in high school. "Prettying up" worked, and I started talking with a boy. Then I finally had a boy who was my "boyfriend" but quickly realized that wasn't really what I wanted.

One of the great things about college for me is that everyone wears sweatpants and Uggs, and no one cares. In middle school and high school, it was all about who had the best smartphones, fashionable clothes, fancy cars, etc. Everyone acted like a pack animal. When they sensed you were different, they cut you out of the pack.

SHARI:

Brittany's social skills were always important but, as I look back, it seems like we first concentrated mostly on physical and educational therapy. I remember when Brittany was little how she had trouble talking to people face-to-face. I knew this was something that autistic kids struggled with, but I refused to let it take control. I would often hold her chin and make her look directly into people's eyes when she was speaking to them to help her learn.

We would meet with family and friends at restaurants, and Brittany would end up turned around in her chair with her back to everyone because she was so afraid of talking to anyone outside the immediate family. We would turn her around and tell her she was not in trouble, but she did need to know that it's rude to turn your back to people.

Over time, she learned how to fake interest and involvement in conversations around her. As she entered her teens, though, we definitely saw the need for something more to help her with social interactions.

That was when we found the PEERS program at UCLA. Admittance required strict adherence to the program. We had to attend every weekly session, with one parent always accompanying Brittany. These requirements were a huge commitment, especially for a single parent. Even though we were divorced, Terry and I shared our concern for supporting Brittany, and he attended most of the sessions as well. In fact, we often would all go to dinner afterward.

Each session started in the late afternoon and lasted two to three hours. The staff separated the kids from the adults, who went into separate rooms for individualized training. Parents and participants would all get back together at the end of the evening.

Brittany had a choice of joining one of two age groups: 18 and younger or 18 and older. At 17, she was on the cusp. She chose the 18 and younger group. Even though that made her one of the oldest in the group, she knew she didn't have the emotional maturity to handle a lot of the subject matter that the older group would address, and she felt much more comfortable working with the younger teens and tweens.

During their sessions, the kids learned about and practiced many of the skills they needed to socialize with everyone from their peers to their teachers to their family and friends. They role-played through many different scenarios, demonstrating and then having the kids practice with the group at large and with each other in pairs.

They learned skills that so many of us develop naturally in life – things such as initiating friendships, having a conversation without interrupting and calling someone on the phone. One entire session was about joking. Kids on the autism spectrum have a lot of trouble telling and understanding jokes and with joking and sarcasm in general. It's so difficult that PEERS dedicated a whole session to the subject.

PEERS also taught students how to initiate a conversation, then step back and ask questions, thus developing more needed social skills. The kids were assigned to work with a partner on skills such as phone conversations outside of class. When we came back the next week, we would talk about the skill again.

This experience was invaluable in preparing Brittany for college. I just wish we had done it a few years earlier, when she was entering high school.

Chapter
8.

If There Are So Many of Us, Why Do I Feel So Alone?

One out of every 50 children in the United States is diagnosed with autism. That means there are millions of parents out there dealing with the same things I am. So why do I feel so alone?

When Brittany was first diagnosed, I didn't know anyone else who had a child with autism. I felt incredibly alone and isolated. All of the social activities I took Matthew to, such as Mommy and Me or Gymboree, didn't work for Brittany. Oh, I tried. I took her to all of those classes and get-togethers. But she was absolutely miserable, and I didn't have a clue why.

Thinking back, I understand now that she wasn't able to handle the stimulation. It was overwhelming. When all of the other kids would run out on the mat during a Gymboree class and start doing tumbles, Brittany would be pounding on the door trying to get out. The other mothers would just stare at her (or me), wondering what was going on and why I wasn't doing anything about it.

I felt so embarrassed and inadequate and had no idea what to do. I couldn't console her. I couldn't figure out what was wrong or why she seemed to hate it so much there when all the other kids were having fun. So I stayed home. And I was lonely.

I didn't feel like anyone understood. They didn't know the pain I was going through. I felt alienated by the other mothers who did all the traditional things such as mommy groups and play dates at the park.

The crying didn't help things, either. When Brittany was first diagnosed, I cried a lot. I didn't want to cry in front of other people, so I stayed home. I didn't feel like I could talk about it with the other moms I knew. I didn't even know how I would start a conversation like that, or what to say or when to say it. If I stayed home, I was safe. Brittany didn't talk until she was around 4 years old, so staying at home meant that I was surrounded by silence as well. Play dates were out of the question.

I left a career I loved to focus on my children. My marriage was falling apart. I felt like there were two battles going on in my life – the divorce and my fight with autism for my child. I lost weight, felt manic, didn't sleep and didn't eat. And I was still crying all the time. I probably should have sought help, but I didn't have the time or the money. Soon after the divorce, my ex-husband stopped paying alimony and child support for two years. I had to reach out to my parents and my sister for help. I carried tremendous guilt, felt very alone and was emotionally drained.

I think it's a common misconception that it's the kids who feel lonely in these situations. Far from it. Brittany was never lonely. She had me. I became everything to her: mother, friend, teacher, therapist, cook, play date, you name it. She always had me to turn to so that she never felt lonely. I became her best friend. We did everything together all the time. It was a sacrifice I made with my eyes wide open. I knew that one day she would move on, and I would be alone.

I was constantly surrounded by therapists and doctors. I didn't talk to them about how I was feeling, and I should have. My doctors never said anything to me about support groups, but 18 years ago there weren't support groups like there are now. So I didn't have that to turn to. I was simply exhausted, and nothing helped me feel better... until I started exercising. It was just the therapy I needed.

I took Pilates and yoga. I learned healing exercises that helped me live in the moment, clear my mind and release the stress. Exercise became my solace. I was able to tune out at the gym – release all of that anxiety, tension and sadness. Day and night, my mind was constantly racing, thinking and worrying about the past, the future and what was right around the corner. Working out helped clear my mind and calm my nerves. And it made me think about eating healthy, too, which is so important.

The burnout rate for parents of special-needs kids is high; we need every bit of emotional and physical help we can get. Poor nutrition and lack of exercise will turn a stressful situation into a dire one. I wish someone had told me this earlier instead of my having to figure it out the hard way.

The biggest piece of advice I'll give for parents of special-needs kids is to make time to do at least one thing every day that makes you feel good. Do your nails, exercise, talk to a friend, pull out your yoga mat and strike some poses in the garden. Anything that helps you feel that you did good and were productive at the end of the day.

The breakdown of my marriage only added to my feelings of isolation. There were good days and bad days with Terry in the early days of Brittany's diagnosis. But the bad days pretty soon started outnumbering the good.

After the first appointment with Dr. Sandra Kaler, a Ph.D. in counseling and mental health who did the initial assessment and analysis on Brittany, we drove home in total silence. He didn't want to talk about it. So I sat in silence, with tears running down my face. Soon after, we started playing the blame game. Who has mental illness in the family? Whose fault is it? Was it because he was an older dad?

Dealing with Brittany, her appointments and her therapies every day used up all of my patience. When Terry came home from work, I was well into overwhelmed mode – yelling, crying and unable to function. So many things bothered me back then. Terry and I never talked about it. We both should have gone to therapy.

I remember Dr. Kaler once said, "Don't ever lose each other, because the moment you lose each other, it's over." Terry was not a communicator at heart. I needed to talk... I HAD to talk. He hated talking. How do you stay together if you can't communicate?

I left Terry in 2005, but our divorce wasn't final until 2010. Matthew, Brittany and I settled in Thousand Oaks, a short ride to the south and closer to Los Angeles and the Valley, where a lot of our doctors and appointments were.

Matthew was miserable. He was 12, and everything was changing. I was so focused on Brittany that I didn't think about how the divorce and moving from a multimillion-dollar beach house to a small rental in a new town and new school would affect him. I enrolled him in a basketball program, but my focus was on transitioning Brittany to a new school with new teachers and making sure she was supported at school and at home.

I was sad a lot. After the divorce, I felt beaten down. The stress, the sadness, the hatred for the person I once was in love with – they all took a big toll on me.

I cried all the time, and I know my kids saw it. I can't imagine what that did to them.

Matthew was having trouble adjusting, and I really wanted to be there for the kids, so I put my social life on hold. I made a lot of sacrifices. I was never angry with them.

Life still felt very lonely. My family lived in Arizona; my best friend was in Chicago. But I'm luckier than most. They were supportive and wonderful and came to visit as often as they could. If I hadn't had them all those years ago, I wouldn't be here today, doing as well as I am.

While exercise saved my sanity, it was family and friends who truly helped me deal with the loneliness and stress of parenting a child with autism. A great group of friends and family can be the ultimate solace. Don't take them for granted.

My first instinct was to shut everyone out when I found out about Brittany's autism. I didn't think they would understand or relate. This was totally new territory. I had no idea how to talk about what I was going through. And I worried that even if I did talk to them, maybe they wouldn't want to hear it. I didn't want to be a burden. Bottom line, with all of these thoughts roaming around in my head, I withdrew from society for a while.

If you feel this way or find yourself thinking like I did, just stop! It's important to talk to your family and friends. Let them know how you're feeling. Give them permission to be open and honest with you. It's a two-way street, and you both have to honor the fact that sometimes you'll need to talk, and sometimes it may all be too much. Friendships are too important to your sanity and survival to neglect.

When Terry and I separated, my sister Lori, her husband and my parents all stepped in to support us. My sister Stacy gave me spiritual guidance and helped me get through with my spirit intact. Lori and her husband flew in for court dates and helped me review papers and get through the divorce and everything that came after. My nephew Adam was like a best friend to the kids and me. He hung out with us and helped the kids get out and have a life when I probably wouldn't have.

Then there was Julie, my best friend since we were young. We've been each other's rock throughout our lives and have always been there for each other. When Brittany was a toddler and we were still trying to figure out what was going on with her, Julie called to tell me that her husband, David, was terminally ill and fading fast. It wasn't a question of if I would go to her, but how fast I could get there.

I flew to Chicago and stayed by their side in the hospital for more than two weeks. David finally told me to go home to my family in California; I had a 2- and 3-year-old waiting for me. Sensing my hesitation, David said, "Don't worry, we'll see each other again some day." I said my goodbyes and flew home. He passed away soon after.

I flew back to Chicago for David's funeral, then back to California again. I was exhausted, worried about Brittany (we hadn't received her diagnosis yet), worried about Julie and dealing with profound grief over losing David. I was overwhelmed with sadness, scrambling to provide the support and love that I knew my friend needed right then. I was ready to count that as one of the worst days of my life.

It was then that I received the news that Brittany had autism. I called Julie, sobbing. Then Julie started sobbing. There was more crying than talking going on, but we were doing it together, and that's what mattered.

When we both calmed down a bit, I felt horrible because I assumed she was crying for David, while I had selfishly been thinking of my own problems. But she was crying for me and for Brittany. I'll never forget her saying, "David and I had a wonderful life together, and I'm so grateful for that. But you're just getting started. And I'm grieving for you and Brittany and what I know you'll have to go through in the years ahead."

So I cried for her. And she cried for me. And we talked and listened and planned and dreamed and were just there for each other. That was the first glimmer of how important it would be for me to have a support system to make it through this next stage of my life.

For me, it's always been important to have girlfriends, sisters of the heart, people who help you, support you and are always there for you. It's finding the right people to work with, the right support system and the right mindset to keep pushing forward, even when life seems like it keeps pushing you back. I know the universe is telling me that where I am is where I'm meant to be and to trust that this is the right place for me.

Chapter
9.

A Business and Life I Love:
Shari's Story

I always thought I was destined to be in show business. I worked as a child and later as a teen model when I was in Chicago. After college, I wanted to learn the business of show biz, so I went to the modeling agency that represented me as a child and asked Shirley Hamilton, owner of Shirley Hamilton Agency, to hire me.

It was the mid-'80s, and there were a lot of movies filming in the Chicago area, including *Ferris Bueller's Day Off, Sixteen Candles, Risky Business, The Breakfast Club* and *About Last Night.* I was thrown to the wolves and had to learn very quickly, as I really knew nothing about casting, production, negotiations, etc.

Because I loved it so much, I learned quickly. Plus, I loved the art of the schmooze. I realized that if I was going to make it, I needed to head west. I remember well-known producer Jon Avnet (*Fried Green Tomatoes*, *Risky Business*, *Black Swan*) telling me, "If you're going to be serious about the entertainment business, you've got to get out to California."

I had very little money, as Shirley Hamilton paid me very little during my time with her agency. So I headed as far west as Arizona, where my family lived. I lived with my parents and got a job working at another modeling agency doing styling jobs for *Phoenix Magazine*, random photo shoots and makeup for Stetson Hats events. Even though I had my cosmetology license and was really good at styling and makeup artistry, I wasn't happy. My sister Lori shoved $200 into my hands and told me to go find my dream in California.

I took a job in the Talent Agency Training Program in Los Angeles, working for no money. I had to supplement my income by working as a cosmetics sales girl at a department store. I made more money on the weekends than I did all week!

I worked my ass off. I never partied so hard or worked so hard. Seven days a week with no breaks, ever. It was the best time of my life. I worked at Canon Films and at Lawrence and Chuck Gordon's Production Company at 20th Century Fox. It was amazing! I was there during the summer blockbuster movies of the late '80s – movies such as *Die Hard, Field of Dreams, Family Business* and *Water World.*

That experience taught me to develop a thick skin that has served me well throughout life. And I mean Teflon thick! After working in the industry and making it this far, I could take pretty much anything thrown my way. There was yelling, men making passes at me, crazy schedules, dealing with creative divas, being treated like crap and anything else that people liked to call "paying my dues."

I met Terry in 1989, and we got married in 1990. I moved to Ventura, left the movie business and was bored out of my mind! I tried my hand at producing a few projects of my own and was very close to producing a TV movie, but things fell through at the eleventh hour. By this time, I had my son, Matthew, and 12 months later I had Brittany. Years later, with a divorce behind me and the desire to support myself and my children, I looked for something new.

I started working in the food business in 2006, right after I left Terry and filed for divorce. My father had been diagnosed with celiac disease, an autoimmune disorder that causes the body's immune system to attack the small intestine whenever the person eats something with gluten. People with celiac must maintain a strict gluten-free diet. Even crumbs can trigger internal damage. People were still new to living gluten-free back then, and my father and I recognized the opportunity.

My father, a founding member of the Celiac Sprue Association (CSA), asked me to start a gluten-free food business with him. I told him I knew nothing about the food business, that my experience was in the movie industry, but we decided to go for it anyway. We called the business Gluten-Free and Fabulous.

During those first few years, I learned a lot about how NOT to run a business. We should have hired a consultant who knew the industry, logistics, all the things we were clueless about back then. Instead, we were just throwing money into a business without knowing what we were doing.

While it looked like we were doing a lot of business, there were no profits at all. In fact, money was disappearing quickly. I discovered that our other partner was issuing purchase orders and bundling inventory to make it look like we were doing business when we really weren't.

Around that time, I had a pretty horrific ski accident. I'm a pretty strong skier. I've skied all over the world, jumped out of helicopters and never had a problem until this time.

We were at Mammoth Ski Resort in California, and it was an incredibly strong, blustery, windy day. We had no business being on that mountain; conditions were too rough. We rode the ski lift up, jumped off and skied to the side to get started down. I was hit by a strong gust as I stood near the edge of a steep cliff. The wind was so powerful that it literally moved me over the edge, where I fell about 600 feet.

They say I survived because I was knocked unconscious at the start. My body was like a rag doll. It was a miracle that no bones were broken, but I had managed to break just about every blood vessel in my body.

I was literally black and blue from head to toe and in extreme pain for weeks. I ended up with years of excruciating back pain. Because of the damage from the fall, I had bones rubbing on bones in my spine. The pain worsened until I couldn't walk.

I finally found a phenomenal spinal surgeon in Southern California who operated on my neck and back. They had to do a C-3 neck fusion and then, six months later, do a fusion laminectomy with a cadaver part on L-4, S-1. I had a ruptured disk at T-12, L-1, which can't be fixed because it's too dangerous. I spent a lot of time laid up during the next two years trying to get back to normal, thus losing touch with the business.

My father brought two schmucks in who talked him into investing even more money in the business. They decided that we should make pizza – a decision I wasn't consulted on at all. They invested in a rundown factory, creating something they didn't know anything about. These guys fast-talked my father into putting up his savings, then used the money to support their lifestyles instead of putting it into the business.

I remember lying in a hospital bed, recuperating and going over bills, when I finally figured out what was going on. At that point, it was too late. These two schmucks who had been put in charge had embezzled a lot of money – all while blaming me for anything and everything that went wrong. I was the young pup and the only woman. My father knew nothing of what was going on. I made the decision to leave the company and close it down. My father and I resigned as members of the LLC we had formed for that business.

Two years later, I knew there was still opportunity in the market for gluten-free foods. I resolved to start over, creating Simply Shari's from scratch. It hasn't been easy. I had no money and had to work hard to scrape up enough to get started. I begged buyers to give me another chance. I had to meet with them in person to explain what happened with the former business and then convince them that my new venture was a viable, attractive and stable opportunity.

It was a rough time. My sister Lori was diagnosed with breast cancer, and I made it a point to be there for her like she was always there for me. Yes, she has a husband, but there's nothing like sisterly love. I flew back and forth from California to Phoenix to be with her throughout her chemotherapy, all while trying to get my business off the ground and take care of my family.

My sister's breast cancer and launching a new business definitely took a toll on me. At times it felt devastating. I've been through so many obstacles, and I'm sick of hearing people tell me that "God must be giving me all these trials in life because I've got big shoulders."

Honestly, a lot of days I feel like it's too much, and I desperately wish for a reprieve. But I also have hope and pray that tomorrow, next month and next year will be better. Experience has taught me that life does go on. My sister's healthy now, everything's getting back on track, and I feel really optimistic about the future.

I've been knocked down so many times, it's a miracle I'm still here and still standing. What's interesting is that my story is helping me succeed. In my business, it's not just about the product, it's about the story behind the product. When I approached buyers for Whole Foods, they were attempting to choose from more than 40 different gluten-free mac-and-cheese products. When they chose Simply Shari's, I asked why. Their answer? My story!

What I've been through, the inspiration of my father and my daughter in starting this business, what I've overcome and how I'm still fighting onward... that resonates with people. And it confirms my earlier thought that I'm here for a reason. I realize that I've finally gotten rid of the bad and kept the good in my life. I'm running a business my way, on my own, providing gluten-free products that are making a difference in the lives of people who really need it.

Chapter

10.

"You Should Be Proud..."

BRITTANY:

I try to never regret the past or do things that would make me regret the past. Be positive, be supportive, be nice, and you never have to regret anything in your life. There are moments where I felt like I should have been more open about how I was feeling, like during my parents' divorce, but I wasn't emotionally ready to be more open. That's probably why I developed the hair-pulling habit.

So I guess it's about learning to express yourself and communicate how you're feeling. My brother was great at letting people know how he felt about things. I internalize, which isn't good. I never really let people know how I felt because I wasn't sure how I felt and didn't know to express it. Sometimes I couldn't feel anything, and I think that's when the stimming started. It gave me the sensory feelings I was looking for, something to feel, so I didn't feel left out by feeling nothing.

Overall, though, I've always tried to be upbeat and optimistic. My middle name is Joy, and I've always tried to be filled with joy. Even looking back at my parents' relationship and what happened between them, I was never mad at my dad, because he's my dad. He has supported and loved me. Now that I'm an adult, I realize that I just need to learn from what others have done and make my own path.

I want to meet a guy, have a relationship, have kids and make my life the way I want it. I've always wanted that. I want to work my way up in my professional field, do work that I'm passionate about and find that guy along the way. I'm not in a hurry, but I'm excited about what's to come.

SHARI:
I wish I could go back to "Shari 1996" and tell her to throw the books away, dry the tears, ignore the naysayers and grab onto hope because – no matter what they say – things will work out. Your children become what you make of them. If you put the work in, you'll come out with great kids.

When people ask me what one thing has helped Brittany and me make it through the years, I tell them communication. From the very beginning, I always taught my kids how to stand up and speak for themselves. I encouraged them to discuss what was going on in their lives, how they were feeling, what was bothering them and how to work through it all. I created the habit for them early, and it worked, as we've always known that we can sit down and discuss anything with each other.

Sometimes encouraging the kids to speak up for themselves created funny situations. When Brittany was younger, we went to see a production of Wicked at the Pantages. We were all settled in and, right as the lights were about to go down, a tall woman with very big hair sat right in front of Brittany, blocking her view. Before I could react, Brittany tapped the woman on her shoulder and politely asked her to move so that she could see. I held my breath, waiting for a rude reaction. The woman stood up, looked at Brittany, leaned over to me and said, "You should be proud of that child" as she scooted over one seat. To this day, that memory makes me smile. I wanted to tell her, "Oh, you have no idea!"

Before Brittany headed off to college, we were in one of our deep discussions, and I asked her if she blamed me for disrupting her life with the divorce and moving. I was still beating myself up over that, carrying that guilt around for years, like only a mom can do. Brittany brought me to tears when she said no, that looking back she could see that without those moves, she never would have found her passion for animation or her art mentor, Sheldon Borenstein. She never would have had her dog, Max, or her horse, Cooper, or the joy of riding competitively and the satisfaction of winning ribbons on her own.

And she was mature and insightful enough to know that without all of that, she may not have been where she is now, graduating from a four-year university with a major in Animation/Digital Media and a minor in Art History, pursuing her true passion in life. Her ability to see the positive and celebrate her successes helped push the guilt I was feeling aside – replaced with warmth, love and pride.

She'd succeeded. One of my main goals for Brittany's life was to bring her to a point where, without actively guiding her, she could function and support herself.

During her time at Chapman University, she received a scholarship to go to Italy for one month to study art history and film in Rome. She traveled with a roommate. They weren't able to find a youth hostel to stay in, so they stayed at a convent. They wandered around on their free time, took trains, ate new foods and had a wonderful experience. The next year it was France. She wanted to study abroad during the second semester of her sophomore year. She applied and was accepted. She ended up interning at the Cannes Film Festival.

I pushed Brittany her whole life. I supported her, but I never let her back down from challenges. If I'd held her back and smothered or protected her too much, none of these experiences would have been possible. Now, seeing her break free and stride forward on her own is the greatest reward.

BRITTANY:
It's all about perseverance.

I personally feel that this is a very important quality to have. Striving for something and then achieving it and looking back on what you did and what you were thinking and then saying, "Wow! I did that! That was all me!"

How does this relate to autism? It relates because I have had to persevere all of my life. I have had to prove people wrong every step of the way. "Oh, I don't know if your daughter will be able to handle a regular four-year college or be able to get into one." PFFFFTT! I'M DOING IT RIGHT NOW! I got deferred from USC! (I chose Chapman University, by the way,) USC! There are people out there who are not autistic and didn't even get THAT! That just means that I get to say to all those people who told me I couldn't do it: "In your face! Do not underestimate autistic people!"

I personally feel it's good to have long-term goals for autistic children. My parents always involved me in a sport or activity to keep me physically active and challenge me to try new things. This was good because I had something to strive for—goals to keep in mind that, once reached, I knew I could do those things on my own. In the long run, striving toward goals as a child has helped with so many other challenges as I grew up and attended college. It was OK for my parents to help me along the way, of course. Everyone needs a little help, autistic or not, but I'm also glad that they gave me the space to try to do some things on my own.

When someone tells you that you can't or won't succeed in something just because of a disability, smack that fool upside the head! Really, don't listen to them. If you really work hard and believe that you can do it, anything is possible. Really it is! Persevere! Strive to do something great and prove those naysayers wrong! That goes for autistic and non-autistic people!

When I was in Israel, there was a moment when our group was around a fire, and we were asked to write about a moment in our lives that had a huge impact, changed us or something like that. I wrote, "Getting into a four-year university." Then I explained why.

I told all of those people gathered around the fire that, because I'm autistic, people didn't think I could function at a regular college. They told me maybe if I was lucky, I could make it at a two-year college. I remember when I heard that, I slapped my hands on the table and told them that I was going to a four-year college no matter what they said!

I've had to struggle and fight my whole life to get where I am, and being accepted into a four-year college was the moment that I achieved my goals and made my mom and dad's dreams come true, as well. It was definitely a life-changing moment. After I spoke, everyone got to their feet and clapped and congratulated me. It was an awesome moment.

SHARI:

I look at Brittany and see a young woman who has beaten all the odds. She has surpassed all expectations. She is not normal – she has surpassed all that is normal and created a life filled with joy and possibility.

Parenting never really ends but, as I watched Brittany throw her cap in the air as she graduated from Chapman this year, I felt a huge sense of accomplishment—like my job is pretty much done. When she was young and we faced that autism diagnosis, my biggest goal was to help Brittany become self-sufficient—to have the ability to do what she needed to live on her own. Watching her graduate and thinking back on the past few years of her college experience, traveling, adventures and achievements, I feel like I can finally put a big check mark next to that goal. Done!

People with special-needs kids tend to think only of the worst when they first face a diagnosis. I know I did. I hope, though, that this book shares my message of hope with you. Hold on to hope, find the joy in life and persevere. Face down the doom and gloom, stop worrying about the future, learn to live in the moment, and celebrate the daily miracles too many people often overlook.

YOU CAN DO IT.
YOUR CHILD CAN DO IT.

And remember: You're not alone.

Chapter
11.

A Mother's Tribute
(Brittany's Graduation)

It's been a long, joyous, often tearful, definitely emotional journey getting Brittany to where she is today. I was so proud to present this tribute to her on the night of her graduation:

2015 DODGE SCHOOL OF FILM, CHAPMAN UNIVERSITY

My Darling Daughter:
I am so very proud of you on this momentous day. I cannot believe four years have gone by so quickly, and you have accomplished so much. When no one except

your father and I had faith that you could attend a four-year university, you showed them! I always taught you that there is no such word as CAN'T – the words we use are I CAN and I WILL. And you did. You attended a four-year university and graduated in four years, as well. People like you and me have to fight harder, study harder and be aggressive in what we want in order to achieve our dreams. And that's OK because it means you're focused on your goals and have passion for what you believe in.

For instance, during your freshman year, you spent the summer living in Italy to study art history/film. Then in the south of France during your sophomore year, you traveled throughout the country and conquered Paris all by yourself. Your independence absolutely blows me away! I was in awe of your bravery when you traveled by bus and plane by yourself to meet Matthew and me in London at one point. Your independence is to be admired.

Your talent is exceptional. As we screened your senior thesis animation film, "Hangry Raccoon," I was overjoyed-kvelling. Afterwards, when you went on stage and spoke so eloquently, I wanted to jump up and scream to the world, "Look, everyone! Look what my daughter has done! She's got such talent!"

You are a perfectionist, and we can see that in your work. You are brilliant and artistic. Your attention to detail, your drive and your focus are to be admired.

I want you to know that you are my dream that came true. The first time I laid my eyes on you, I knew you were meant for greatness. It took a lot of hard work, some disappointments and a lot of love, and we did learn that it does indeed take a village to help a family with a special-needs child. But look at you... You are so beautiful, so sweet, so honest and so loving. What more could a parent ask for?

You and I are joined at the hip; we have a special bond. I know when you need me, and I know when to let you fly on your own. We've had amazing moments together. You are the best traveler and know so much that I feel like the student, and you're my teacher. I taught you how to cook, and now you're the gourmet cook in the family. And now Nanny and I will be traveling with you to Salzburg, Germany. We are so excited to share in this journey with three generations.

Your love for the arts, reading, theater and the movies is so wonderful, as most young adults have no interest in what I feel are the greatest creations on Earth. It's just one of the many wonderful things that sets you apart as being so well rounded and diverse.

Don't ever stop being a student of life; you'll keep learning to the end. A new chapter of your life begins tomorrow after graduation. Soak it all in, and cherish these great memories you're making, as the best is yet to come!

I love you so much, baby girl.

Love,

Mom

RESOURCES

Americans with Disabilities Act:
www.ada.gov

Brittany's Blog:
http://autisticgirl15.blogspot.com/

Brittany's Twitter:
@britters1516 (www.twitter.com/britters1516)

Brittany's artist site:
www.cole131.wix.com/britbritboom

Brittany's YouTube:
https://www.youtube.com/user/SuperBrittCole

Celiac Support Association /
Celiac Sprue Association (CSA):
http://www.csaceliacs.org/index.jsp

Celiac Disease Foundation (CDF):
http://celiac.org/

Simply Shari's Gluten Free:
http://www.simplysharis.com/

Autism Speaks:
www.autismspeaks.org

Talk About Curing Autism:
www.TACAnow.org

Tri-Counties Regional Center serving Santa Barbara, Ventura & San Luis Obispo Counties:
http://www.tri-counties.org/

UCLA PEERS Program:
http://www.semel.ucla.edu/peers

University of California, Santa Barbara Koegel Autism Center:
http://education.ucsb.edu/autism

Dr. Sandra Kaler, PhD:
860 Via de la Paz,
Pacific Palisades, CA 90272
(310-454-9998)

Autism Society of America:
http://autismla.org/

Foothill Autism Alliance:
http://www.foothillautism.org/

Family Focus Empowerment Center:
http://www.familyfocusresourcecenter.org/

Wright's Law:
http://www.wrightslaw.com/

TASK – Team of Advocates for Special Kids:
http://www.taskca.org/

Mental Health Advocacy Services:
http://www.mhas-la.org/

NEA: Teaching Students with Autism
(A Guide for Educators):
http://www.nea.org/home/18459.htm

NEA: Individuals with Disabilities
Education Act (IDEA) resources:
http://www.nea.org/home/18704.htm

Understanding Individualized
Education Programs (IEPs):
https://www.understood.org/en/school-learning/
special-services/ieps/understanding-individualized-
education-programs

Parent guide to the Family Education
and Rights Act (FERPA):
https://www2.ed.gov/policy/gen/guid/fpco/
brochures/parents.pdf